# Three Plays

*three full-length stage plays*

## Duane Kelly

Special thanks to Edward Albee, and all the fine members of the id/Seven Devils theater family.  And most especially, to Alice.

*The Thing With Feathers* benefitted from development at the 2009 Seven Devils Playwrights Conference in McCall, Idaho, and from a reading at Lark Play Development Center in New York.  *A Dying Wish* and *Future Imperfect* benefitted from readings produced by id Theater in New York.

# Table of Contents

# A Dying Wish

a play by

## DUANE KELLY

## CHARACTERS

IRIS, 48, dying of ovarian cancer
LEW, 49, her husband
MEG, 17, their daughter (at rebellious stage)
DIDGE, 46, neighbor (good-hearted, scatterbrained)
FRAN, 37, Iris's sister

## TIME

Mid-August 2002

## PLACE

A large living room of a comfortable middle-class house in Seattle. A hospital bed has been temporarily set up, positioned for a view to the garden. Strung above the bed are festive letters spelling "WELCOME HOME MOM." Miscellaneous living room furniture and a wheelchair. A full 3-ring Notebook with page dividers is visible. This Notebook remains visible throughout play. Only other set is one scene on a train station bench.

# *ACT 1*

## SCENE 1

*(Dusk, Wednesday, mid-August 2002, light rain outside. Asleep in the hospital bed is IRIS, having recently returned home for her final days. She is dying of ovarian cancer. Her friend and neighbor DIDGE has been tidying up, is now cleaning up spill on Iris's blanket. LEW is sitting reading Notebook.)*

DIDGE: I'm afraid I've made a mess.

LEW: *(distracted)* What's that?

DIDGE: A mess. Not a big one. You have enough worries don't you without me spilling soup?

LEW: No need to cry over spilt soup.

DIDGE: Oh, it's just chicken broth which should come out in the wash. I'll wait until she wakes up to take care of it.

LEW: I don't expect her to sleep for long. The pain. She's refusing to take morphine during the day.

DIDGE: Well, it'll be night soon enough. I'll need to use your laundry room though.

LEW: Our laundry room? Of course.

DIDGE: I'm sorry but mine's out of commission. This idiot of a contractor redoing my kitchen - I wish I had never started - his guys busted water pipes so now they've shut off the water to the house. For a little while.

LEW: That's too bad.

DIDGE:  At least they say "for a little while".

LEW:  We can hope.

DIDGE:  Remember I made you a sandwich.  It's in the fridge.

LEW:  A sandwich.

DIDGE:  Chicken salad.

LEW:  Must be the day for chicken.

DIDGE:  Want me to get it for you?

LEW:  Thanks, not hungry.

DIDGE:  You should eat something.

LEW:  I'm sure it'll hit the spot later.

DIDGE:  And I made fresh applesauce for the three of you, from my very own apple tree.  They're just starting to ripen.

LEW:  *(distracted)* Malus sauce.

DIDGE:  No, applesauce.

LEW:  Malus domestica.  Genus and species.  Bad, bitter, nasty.  That's the genus of the apple tree.

DIDGE:  Bitter and nasty genius who?  What are you talking about?

LEW:  Ninety-nine percent of apple trees produce fruit so bitter they turn the mouth of Homo sapiens inside out.  The apples you use for your sauce are among the precious few that are edible.

DIDGE:  Oh.

LEW:  Did you add sugar?

DIDGE: A little.

LEW: Probably a good idea. Just in case.

DIDGE: Thank you professor. Everything you're having to deal with, I know it's really tough. When Preston died, all that stuff almost overwhelmed me. If it hadn't been for you and Iris I don't know how I would have survived. Anything I can do to help, I will.

LEW: I know, Didge. Thanks.

DIDGE: It's the least I can do. When there's so much for you to worry about.

LEW: Not as much as you might think. One of the advantages of being married to Iris is that she takes care of most everything.
*(Starts to open Notebook; hesitates as suspicion occurs to him that Didge already knows its contents)*
Have you seen this?

DIDGE: No. What is it?

LEW: Well I'm still sorting it out. Iris appears to have put in here everything Meg and I need. She's filled up the car, bought the maps and planned Meg's and my journey. All I have to do is settle in behind the wheel. She's got everything in here - doctors, dentists, mechanics, plumbers, lawyers, insurance agent, important dates.

DIDGE: Butcher, baker -

LEW: And undertaker.

DIDGE: I wish someone had done that for me. When I see her now I can't help but think of Preston.

LEW: She's not in the ground yet.

DIDGE: I know. I'm sorry. It just brings back all these memories. . . . I hate to ask you this but can I come back after I feed the cats, for a bath?

LEW: *(indicating IRIS)* Does she need one?

DIDGE: No, for me.

LEW: For you? Oh. Do you need one?

DIDGE: The water. I don't have any, remember?

LEW: Oh. That's right. Sure. That'll be fine.

DIDGE: I'll stay out of your hair. Look Lew I know what an awful time this is for you. I've always felt - so did Preston - that you and Meg and Iris were like family. I want to help you.

*(DIDGE gives LEW a hug. LEW keeps Notebook against him as a barrier. DIDGE senses LEW's discomfort and pulls away.)*

LEW: I'll finish cleaning up.

DIDGE: *(a little hurt)* No, don't you bother. There's not much here. I'll just take these in the kitchen. Things could be worse.

LEW: How's that?

DIDGE: At least you've got water.

LEW: Yes, I do. That's reassuring.

DIDGE: I'll be back in an hour or so. Maybe a half-hour.

*(DIDGE, carrying dishes, bumps IV-stand as she exits. Lew catches it before it falls over.)*

LEW: For the bath?

DIDGE: Yes, that's right.

LEW: See you in a while then.
*(Depressed. Checks watch. Sits down with Notebook. Drinks from glass of wine. Stares into dark)*

## ACT 1, SCENE 2

*(Wednesday evening, one hour later.  Daughter MEG enters through front door, disheveled, slightly injured, slightly drunk.  LEW wakes from sleep in chair, Notebook still in lap.)*

MEG:  *(blithely)* Hi Dad.

LEW:  Oh, hello.  Have you had any dinner?  You should eat.

MEG:  I had a bite with Pete.

LEW:  Let me guess, an Almond Joy, with a Butterfinger for  dessert.

MEG:  No, Dad, you got it backward.  Butterfinger was the main course.  Cheese-burger for an appetizer.

LEW:  Good.  For a minute I was worried about your diet.

MEG:  How's Mom doing?

LEW:  Wrong question.  Where'd you and Pete go?  For your appetizer.

MEG:  Dick's Drive-In.  Up on Holman.

LEW:  Where else did you go?

MEG:  Just driving around.  Dad, I need to talk.

LEW:  Sure.

MEG:  I can't talk to Mom.

LEW:  She'll be up soon.

MEG:  No you.

LEW:  Sure hon.  What's on your mind?

MEG: This school in Montana. I really don't want to go. In fact, I think it'd be a disaster.

LEW: *(puts up his palms, defensively)* Mom's idea. I just found out she's already paid the full-year's tuition. And this school's not cheap, I can tell you.

MEG: Well, I think it's stupid, dumb and a ridiculous idea.

LEW: So you don't like it?

MEG: Mom never even talked to me. I want to stay here, in Seattle, with you. If you make me go, I'm gonna leave.

LEW: Leave?

MEG: Leave.

LEW: Leave? What kind of leave?

MEG: Leave leave. Run away. That kind of leave.

LEW: You're way overreacting. I know Mom did a lot of research. She talked to Christine's mother who told her it was great for Christine.

MEG: Dad, Christine went into rehab last month.

LEW: All your Mom wants is to make sure you're going to be all right. After she's gone.

MEG: I'm not the only one Mom's worried about.

*(LEW turns up light to see MEG better. Notices scraped skin.)*

LEW: What has happened to you? Let me see. Has that boy hit you?

MEG: No, he hasn't hit me.

LEW: I want to know what's happened.

MEG:  I told you, we were just driving around.

LEW:  Young lady?

MEG:  What?

LEW:  Meg!

MEG:  Okay, don't have a cardiac.  Pete had a few beers.  I told him that was enough.  We sort of got in a fight.  He was driving fast, got the car stuck in a ditch.

LEW:  Oh Meg. *(goes to examine her scratches)* Let me look at that.

MEG:  *(feigning reluctance, lets LEW examine her)* It's only a few scratches.

LEW:  *(satisfying himself that her injuries are superficial)* You did walk in on your own power.  So where is wonderboy?

MEG:  In jail.  Arrested.  For a DUI.

LEW:  Meg, Meg, Meg.  Isn't life screwed up enough without you helping it?  I know some boys drink and drive, some do drugs, some even beat up girls.  But did you have to pick the trifecta?

MEG:  I'm doing okay.

LEW:  You are?  I'm too old to remember what it's like being a teenager, but I really doubt that this qualifies as okay.

MEG:  You probably spent all your time in science lab.  Mom says you were born with a microscope.

LEW:  I was, they let me be there, in the delivery room, when you were born.

MEG:  What are we talking about?

LEW:  You.  The subject is how you've descended to your current condition.  Did I ever tell you about that?

MEG: My descending?

LEW: Your getting all tangled up. When you descended down the birth canal.

MEG: Right.

LEW: You were turned the wrong way round and when the doctor was turning you the right way your mother starts hemorrhaging and her blood pressure is dropping. Then the doctor discovers you've got the umbilical cord tangled around your neck and so he decides to do an emergency C-section. For a minute we thought we were losing you both.

MEG: You were there? You never told me that.

LEW: Yes, I was there. Seeing you enter this big scary world.

MEG: Did I cry, the way you always see on TV.?

LEW: As I remember, we were all crying. It was a pretty wet delivery room. (*pause*) You've always demonstrated an amazing ability to get yourself all tangled up.

MEG: Yeah, right, and an even more amazing ability to get untangled.

LEW: According to you. There's a big difference between raging adolescent hormones and -

MEG: Not tonight. I don't need any lecture about boys and love.

LEW: Because you know so much?

MEG: What do you and Mom know about it? When did you really love each other?

LEW: Stupid doesn't look good on you.

MEG: Well when did you?

LEW: It's an imperfectly good marriage. What you don't know yet is that life is constant high-dose radiation and love is the DNA. There may be damage but the DNA's still there.

MEG: So now you're telling me that nuclear fall-out is the reason you and Mom always yap at each other.

LEW: It's a metaphor. Something you'd understand if you'd quit cutting English classes. And it's not yapping, it's healthy debate.

MEG: Just like this, right?

LEW: You'll come to understand these things if you live long enough to get married.

MEG: And what's that supposed to mean?

LEW: That if you keep getting in car wrecks with drunken delinquents I'll be carrying your casket before I can walk you down the aisle.

MEG: Maybe I'll be cremated like Mom.

LEW: Don't talk like that.

MEG: You're the one who brought it up. I know what love is.

LEW: Sure you do. You're drowning in hormone soup, that's what you're doing.

*(Their arguing wakes up IRIS.)*

IRIS: What are you two banshees yelling about?

LEW: The finer points of love.

IRIS: Well I'm glad Meg found an expert to talk to.

MEG: *(to LEW)* See! *(to IRIS)* Hi Mom. How's the pain?

IRIS: If I felt any better, I'd be dead. You and your Dad shouldn't be fighting.

MEG: Would you talk to him about that? I've got to go clean up. I just got in.

*(MEG exits.)*

IRIS: Where's she come from? She looks a mess.

LEW: She's been out.

IRIS: With Pete?

*(LEW doesn't respond.)*

IRIS: She has, hasn't she? The image of a daughter kissing a rat with an earring in its tongue is enough to put me in the grave.

LEW: She'll be all right.

IRIS: How many rocks did she turn over to find that rodent? *(exhibits pain)*

LEW: The stomach?

IRIS: Everywhere down there. These little bugs with sharp canines and grinding molars, having a feast down there; that's what it feels like.

LEW: I wish you would take some morphine. The doctor said -

IRIS: I still have too much to take care of to be in a fog all the time. I'll take some before the night's over. . . She's going to have to be . . .

LEW: She? Have to be what?

IRIS: Meg. Are you in a fog? She's going to have to find a way. To be tougher. So are you. The next time life throws shit at you, I'm not going to be here.

LEW: Shit?

IRIS: Yes, ca-ca.

LEW: Your vocabulary expanded in the hospital.

IRIS: Damned right it did. How are you two ever going to make it?

LEW: She has your backbone. Under the tatoos.

IRIS: A scared little girl's under that skin. Subcutaneous terror, one of my doctors might call it.

LEW: It's just teenage angst, not bubonic plague. What she's terrified about is losing you.

IRIS: What's wrong with your ear?

LEW: What?

IRIS: The band-aid. *(gestures)*

LEW: Oh. When women hit middle-age do they get this problem?

IRIS: Honey, there's not enough time.

LEW: This morning, when I found my razor, I shaved my ears.

IRIS: Your ears?

LEW: It's frigging ridiculous.

IRIS: Yeah you are.

LEW: No, just my ears. I reach forty-five -

IRIS: Fifty.

LEW: Not fifty yet.

IRIS: Three months, five days.

LEW: A few years back the hair just starts sprouting out of my ears, like horse-tails. What's that all about? Do you have hair sprouting on you?

IRIS: Umm, I think I have the opposite problem.

LEW: Yes, well, I mean, before, were you finding new hair?

IRIS: Like where?

LEW: I don't know, between your toes?

*(IRIS wiggles a foot out of the blanket and examines it.)*

IRIS: No, I don't think so.

LEW: Then what is it with us guys? I study trees that can be three hundred years old and at the one hundred and fifty year mark they don't just all of a sudden start sprouting branches in places where branches never grew.

IRIS: I don't know Lew. Maybe put one of your grad students on it.

LEW: And then I cut my my ear pruning the damn stuff.

IRIS: You poor boy.

*(LEW gives IRIS three wrapped "welcome home" gifts.)*

LEW: Here, these are for you.

IRIS: Presents? For me? Maybe someone gave me hair conditioner. I can use it on my new growth you're worried about. *(picks up the smallest gift)* From Pete? I didn't know rodents gave things.

LEW: Diseases.

IRIS: Oh, that's right; lots of diseases. Maybe I shouldn't open it, my immune system's low. *(opens gift: four fat joints and a book of matches)* How thoughtful. He remembered the matches. *(smells to confirm it's pot; playfully puts it between her lips)* How many years has it been?

LEW: So long I can't remember.

IRIS: Then it must have been good. Isn't that what they say?

LEW: *(points to a gift)* That one's from me.

IRIS: Oh that's sweet honey. Thanks. *(puts the gifts aside)*
I am fading. Do you mind if I open them later? Where's the nurse?

LEW: Gone home for the evening. She'll be back in the morning.

IRIS: And Didge?

LEW: Went home a few minutes ago. The nurse checked your blood pressure.

IRIS: And?

LEW: Excellent, one-thirty over eighty.

IRIS: The perfect picture of health.

LEW: Here are your pills. *(gives IRIS meds)* I think I got them right.

IRIS: Let me see the chart. *(compares pills to instructions on chart)* I'm only supposed to take one of these Seromycin. Here, put this back. *(hands LEW excess pill then holds up a large pill)* I don't think I can swallow this one.

LEW: I'll get you some water.

IRIS: Get K-Y, not water; it's a suppository.

LEW: Oh. We don't want to be swallowing that.

IRIS: You can try. It'll help with nausea if you can get it down.
*(takes her pills)*

LEW: *(picks up Notebook; turns to "Montana School" section)*
You know, this Montana school isn't going over too well.

IRIS: I'll talk to her again. I can bring her around.

LEW: I'm not so sure. Now she's threatening to run away if we follow through with this.

IRIS: I did my homework. It's what she needs.

LEW: Maybe it will do more harm than good.

IRIS: How can it do her harm?

LEW: Taking her away from what she's familiar with, at a time when she's already vulnerable. I don't think she's that troubled. I know she gets in trouble, but I don't think she's troubled, if you see what I mean.

IRIS: Have you gone blind? You're the one who sees trouble everywhere.

LEW: Everywhere?

IRIS: That's right. Cork stuck in the wine bottle, morning paper late, Internet down: it's all trouble to you. And now you don't recognize the real thing when it's staring you in the face.

LEW: A real "troubledor", that's me.

IRIS: That's right, the man who sings trouble.

LEW: Trouble, trouble toil and bubble.

IRIS: That's not it.

LEW: What?

IRIS: Not how it goes.

LEW: I know that.

IRIS: Double, double, toil and trouble. Stick to trees.

LEW: I can take care of Meg.

IRIS: You can't even take care of your ears. Why do you and Meg have to fight me on everything? Who do you think I'm doing this for? I'm checking out in a few days. Do you get that?

LEW: Yes, I get that.

IRIS: Who knows you two better than me?

*(Beat.)*

IRIS: I don't want you to be abandoned and have everything turn into a big mess around here.

*(LEW looks at Notebook again.)*

LEW: There's something else you have in here - this other thing . . .

IRIS: That you need to get a physical once a year?

LEW: You know what I mean. How doped up were you when you got that idea?

IRIS: Look Lew, I've thought this through. You - and Meg - are going to need help.

LEW: Meg's going to be in Montana, remember?

IRIS: Well you're going to need help.

LEW: Will you quit saying that?

IRIS: And Meg will when she comes home from school.

LEW: If, if you wanted me to marry someone else, just maybe you should have said so before we got married.

IRIS: The only reason I'm telling you this is because we are married and in a few days we won't be married. Our marriage will be past tense, past imperfect. Instead of being a brow-beaten husband you'll be a depressed widower. That's why you must do what I say. Didge is already like family. Plus she thinks you're cute.

LEW: How do you know that?

IRIS: She's told me. More than once.

LEW: Has she seen my ears? You don't remarry because of cute.

IRIS: It doesn't hurt.

LEW: These plans of yours, the ones from Mt. Olympus, how much have you told Didge?

IRIS: None. You're going to have to start showing some  initiative.

LEW: Are you sure?

IRIS: I'm sure you need to, but I'm not sure you will.

LEW: *(with increased emphasis)* Have you told Didge? About this?

IRIS: No.

LEW: Iris.

IRIS: All I said is that I was hoping she would stay close to you and Meg, that you two will need some help.

LEW: And what did she say?

IRIS: That I didn't even have to ask. That she was already planning on staying close and helping out.

LEW: Well the whole idea is ridiculous. If you insist on this, then Meg won't be alone when she runs away.

IRIS: Now there's a mature response. The deaf cripple leads the blind dog. Didge and Preston were always like Meg's aunt and uncle.

LEW: And Didge can keep on being her aunt. Don't you think there's just a little bit of kitty litter missing from her catbox?

IRIS: No more than most of us. Well, maybe just a little. But wouldn't it be a relief having a woman around who doesn't keep the spices in alphabetical order?

LEW: Okay, okay, please tell me what are the three parts of Meg's and my life I am going to screw up the most? I'm not talking about locking the keys in the car here. I'm talking big-time, irretrievably mangle beyond recognition.

IRIS: I'm limited to three?

LEW: Stop it. Give me some credit . . . It seems just yesterday, in that rainstorm, that we were taking Meg home from the hospital. I changed her first diaper, remember? I can handle our future.

IRIS: Hmff, the future. It's the hardest thing to predict. *(pause)* I'm worried Meg could fall over the same cliff as my sister.

LEW: Your sister? We don't know, maybe Fran finally landed on her feet.

IRIS: That'll be the day. People don't change Lew. I need to know that you're -

LEW: I know, I know, I know.

IRIS: So it looks like there's no nurse tonight.

LEW: Yes there is. Me. I'm on duty. What can I help you with ma'am?

IRIS: I wish she was here.

LEW: Fran?

IRIS: Don't be ridiculous. The nurse.

LEW: What is it? I can help.

IRIS: No you can't. Oh, I hate this! Hate it, hate it!, HATE IT!

LEW:  What?

IRIS:  *(fighting back tears)* I need to go.

LEW:  Go?

IRIS:  I am going.  But right now, I, I need to . . . pee.

LEW:  Oh.  That.  Well, okay.  I can help.  What do I do?

IRIS:  First get the bedpan.

*(LEW gets spitbowl.)*

IRIS:  No that's what you upchuck in.  The bedpan's that green thing over there.

*(LEW exchanges spitbowl for bedpan.  Gives it to IRIS.)*

LEW:  Now what?

IRIS:  Help me lift up the gown and slide it under.  Now go stand over there.  And look the other way.

*(IRIS adjusts the bedpan.  LEW looks partly away.)*

IRIS:  You're looking.

LEW:  No I'm not.

*(LEW looks fully away.  IRIS discreetly pees.)*

IRIS:  Okay now you can take and flush it down the toilet, then rinse it out.  I'm sorry.

*(LEW does as IRIS instructs.  While LEW is off, IRIS opens his gift - a silk nightgown. IRIS cries, covering her face with nightgown.)*

## ACT 1, SCENE 3

*(Next morning, Thursday. Bed is empty. DIDGE enters with applesauce and open catfood cans. DIDGE notices IRIS is absent. Lew enters from the garden.)*

DIDGE: Oh no. Oh, Lew! I'm so sorry. You should have got me right away.

LEW: *(confused)* It wasn't a problem. I got her outside myself.

DIDGE: Outside!

LEW: But now I can't find the shovel.

DIDGE: What are you doing?

LEW: Nothing, until I find our shovel.

DIDGE: You can't do that!

LEW: Did you borrow it?

DIDGE: Lew, you have to call a funeral home.

LEW: To move some ferns?

DIDGE: Ferns?

LEW: Iris wants me to move two of her maidenhair ferns.

DIDGE: Where, where is Iris?

LEW: Outside, in her garden in the wheelchair. You can see her out there, over by the roses. When she saw that sun this morning, she said she had to have it on her face. It's a beautiful morning out there.

DIDGE: She must be feeling better.

LEW: Good enough to get out of bed and be outside.

DIDGE: Do you think she wants something to eat?

LEW: I think we should let her enjoy the garden. I don't expect her to be out there too long.

DIDGE: I'll just put this in the fridge. Can I put my catfood in there too?

LEW: Catfood?

DIDGE: I really can't believe these idiots working on my house. Can you?

LEW: Don't know them.

DIDGE: Now they've cut off the power as well as the water. I've got some milk and a few other things I'd like to put in your fridge, for a day or so. Is that all right?

LEW: Sure.

DIDGE: I promise I won't bring stuff over I can't recognize. I mean some of that food's been in there way too long.

LEW: I have to warn you, that sort of thing isn't permitted in Iris's fridge. How can you tell?

DIDGE: Tell?

LEW: What's bad.

DIDGE: Oh there are lots of clues. One is if it's changed color.

LEW: Right.

DIDGE: Of course, that assumes you can remember the original color. Another giveaway is mobility.

LEW: Mobility?

DIDGE: That's right.

LEW: In the fridge?

DIDGE: Herr Professor probably knows the answer: Can molds move?

LEW: I do trees, not molds. There are a zillion molds in this world. Who knows?

DIDGE: Sometimes some of that green stuff has moved from where it was the night before. That's probably a sign, don't you think?

LEW: Probably. For a biologist anyway.

DIDGE: Oh well, I can turn moldy lemon into lemonade. Now I have a good excuse to clean out all that crap.

LEW: Excellent idea.

DIDGE: Will you look at this? *(looks at catfood cans and their labels)* My cats are so darned spoiled. Daisy will only eat shrimp and salmon casserole and for Roscoe it's nothing but savory duck in meaty juices. I wish someone would fix me savory duck in meaty juices.

LEW: Someone besides Ralston Purina.

DIDGE: I was thinking more along the lines of Wolfgang Puck.

LEW: I suppose all creatures have their preferences, from molds to cats to us.

DIDGE: Yes I suppose. We certainly do don't we? Maybe sometime . . .

LEW: Yes?

DIDGE: Never mind. It's not important.

LEW: Are you going to be around tomorrow?

DIDGE: Sure. I was planning to stay close, in case, well you know -

LEW: In case -

DIDGE: In case you or Meg or Iris needed me. Why?

LEW: I was just thinking if any visitors come by, we could maybe use your help.

DIDGE: Who might be coming?

LEW: I don't know. Just people might be coming by, like from her law firm or something, to say hello or goodbye or take care of unfinished business; things I might need help with.

DIDGE: Sure, I'll be here. Just holler.

LEW: Thanks. I don't know what to expect.

DIDGE: I understand.

LEW: Preston's been gone more than a year.

DIDGE: Almost a year and a half.

LEW: It was a nice funeral.

DIDGE: Yes it was.

LEW: If a funeral can be said to be nice.

DIDGE: I think they can. You should be grateful for what Iris has done.

LEW: I know.

DIDGE: All that stuff in the Notebook.

LEW: Oh yes, that. You don't know how grateful.

DIDGE: The arrangements almost did me in.

LEW: So you said. I can imagine. All I have to do is dial the numbers.

DIDGE: When the time comes.

LEW: Yes, it is coming.

DIDGE: Unfortunately.

LEW: Regrettably.

DIDGE: But when it does come you can count on me.

LEW: Thank you for that. I liked the woman who sang.

DIDGE: I'm sorry.

LEW: At his funeral.

DIDGE: Oh yes. Beth, from the choir. A beautiful soprano.

LEW: "That saved a wretch like me."

DIDGE: "Was blind but now I see." She often sings the solos at the church.

LEW: Do you still miss him? I mean I know you miss him, I didn't mean that you don't miss him; I was just wondering how you found it dealing with . . all that . . . with everything since, you know.

DIDGE: The best advice I can give you is do your crying in the shower.

LEW: The shower? Now that's helpful.

DIDGE: So your face doesn't swell.

LEW: Oh. Good trick.

DIDGE: It really works. Try it some time.

LEW: Don't want a swollen face.

DIDGE: A swollen heart is bad enough. But just because someone has passed away doesn't mean they're gone completely, forever.

LEW:  I can see how the memories would be a comfort.

DIDGE:  Yes, they are. . . But that's not exactly what I meant.

LEW:  No?

DIDGE:  Sometimes late at night, around the time I'm getting ready for bed, I'll be thinking about Preston.  And then the phone rings, but just once.  I go to answer it but no one's there.

LEW:  *(becoming alarmed)* I can help you bring stuff over to put in the fridge.  The stuff you can recognize.

DIDGE:  Strange, isn't it?

LEW:  Yes, I think you could say that.

DIDGE:  On the other hand maybe it's just not used to being by myself.

LEW:  *(anxious to change the subject)* You can put as much stuff in the fridge as you like.  Even if you don't recognize it.

DIDGE:  Do you think -

LEW:  Yes, I do, the faster we get your milk over here, the better.  Need help?

DIDGE:  No, no, I can manage.  You should go check on Iris.

*(DIDGE exits.  LEW looks outside, then exits to garden.)*


## ACT 1, SCENE 4

*(Next morning, Friday.  LEW is with IRIS, who sleeps in hospital bed.  Doorbell chimes. LEW opens door.  It is Iris's sister FRAN.)*

FRAN:  *(awkwardness)* Hi.  Are you Lew?

LEW:  Yes. Fran? It's Fran, right? It's been a long time.  I didn't know if for sure, or when you'd -

FRAN:  I was able to get an earlier flight that didn't cost a  fortune.

LEW:  You, you've changed.

FRAN:  Well, it's been a really long time.

LEW:  Yes, it has, hasn't it?

FRAN:  I guess everyone changes over that many years.

LEW:  I had more hair back then, that's for sure.  Except on my ears.

FRAN:  What?

LEW:  Nothin'.  It's good to see you.

FRAN:  I tried calling from the airport but no one was answering.

LEW:  I had the phone turned off so it wouldn't wake up -
*(nods toward IRIS, signals to be quiet)*

FRAN:  Good idea.

LEW:  I need to ask you -

FRAN:  Yes? . . . What is it?

LEW:  Well, not to let Iris know I called.

FRAN:  Called?

LEW:  You.

FRAN:  Me?  That you called me?

LEW:  Yes, you.

FRAN:  She doesn't know anything about this?

LEW:  *(sheepishly)* Well, no, I don't think so.

FRAN:  You don't think so?

LEW:  Shh.  Well, no, not really.  There hasn't been the right time yet, see.

FRAN:  How big a fan do you have for this shit to hit?  This is going to be great.

*(Car honks off.)*

FRAN:  Oh, the taxi.

LEW:  I'll take care of it.

*(LEW exits.  FRAN is shocked at IRIS's emaciated condition.  Examines framed photo of Iris, Lew and Meg.  LEW returns with suitcase.  Accidentally slams the door and then drops the suitcase, waking IRIS.  FRAN ducks out of IRIS's sight.)*

IRIS:  What's happening?

LEW:  Nothing dear.

IRIS:  I was having this god-awful nightmare.

LEW:  Everything's okay now.

IRIS:  What channel have you been watching?

LEW:  Looks like we might get some rain.

IRIS:  *(looking at the sky)* We have to pay for yesterday's good weather.  Then again, those clouds could break up.

LEW:  I was outside earlier.  Feels like rain to me.

IRIS:  Did you water the ferns?

LEW: Righto. Umm, guess who's here?

IRIS: Well, I'm still here, for the moment anyway. You're here. Presumably Meg hasn't run away yet.

LEW: Not the last time I checked.

IRIS: What do you mean here?

LEW: Guess who's come to visit.

IRIS: How would I know?

LEW: Someone you haven't seen for a really really long time.

IRIS: I may not have enough time left for "Twenty Questions".

LEW: Okay, it's your sister.

IRIS: What do you mean my sister?

LEW: Your sister's come for a visit.

IRIS: For a visit? Here?

LEW: Your sister Francine, from Baltimore -

IRIS: I know where she lives.

LEW: Well she's here.

IRIS: Oh, god, that was my nightmare. Fran is not supposed to set foot in this house; you know that. She's supposed to keep her crises on the East Coast. What is going on Lew?

LEW: I told you. Your sister's here to visit.

IRIS: She just happened to drop by?

LEW: That's right. It's a free country. People can travel.

IRIS: I don't suppose she got a call from anyone.

LEW: What? I know how you feel about Fran. . . . And you didn't put her number in the Notebook.

IRIS: So you were looking for it.

LEW: No, I was not looking for it.

IRIS: You're not joking are you? This is just great. I know - maybe if I pretend to be sick she won't stay long. Dammit to hell. So where is she?

LEW: Well, she's not here, as you can see.

IRIS: Lew, don't do this.

LEW: Not right here anyway.

IRIS: You just said she was here.

LEW: That was before I said she wasn't here. I don't see her right now. Do you?

IRIS: Is my sister here or not?

*(FRAN steps into IRIS's view.)*

FRAN: Hello Iris.

LEW: Hello Fran. I was just telling Iris you weren't here. Glad you could pay us a visit.

IRIS: *(to LEW)* Why are you glad?

LEW: A little bit anyway. Aren't you?

IRIS: Not even a little. *(to FRAN)* We had an agreement.

FRAN: I know. Don't think I've forgotten. But isn't this what you lawyers call an extenuating circumstance?

IRIS: No. Unless you mean "extenuating" as in "diminishing." Yes, "diminishing" would be a polite way to describe my condition. If you mean "extenuating" as in "justifying your presence", the answer is no.

FRAN: Do you have to do this?

IRIS: What? Oh I know. *(to LEW)* We need to be gentle with Fran. She's had a difficult life.

FRAN: You know what. Exactly this crap. You still have to be Miss Smarty Pants after all these years.

IRIS: Okay, tell us, Miss Wild Panties, what do you need this time?

FRAN: I'm not here because I need anything.

IRIS: The only time I've heard from you is when you've needed something, usually money.

FRAN: Don't.

IRIS: Don't what?

FRAN: Can you hear yourself? What a cheap shot that was? My god, the last time we talked was on the phone some fucking ten years ago.

IRIS: You don't have to swear. And years don't fuck.

LEW: Umm, while you two are getting reacquainted I'll go make sure Didge is okay in the kitchen.

IRIS and FRAN: You don't need to go.

LEW: Yes I do. Something about crossed wires causing sparks. In the kitchen. I'll be right back.

*(LEW exits.)*

FRAN: Who's Didge? What's she doing in your kitchen?

IRIS: Didge is our neighbor. And I think he means her kitchen, not ours. Then why'd you come?

FRAN: How are you? It doesn't look too good, does it?

IRIS: *(running hand over scalp)* No it doesn't. I need to find a different salon.

FRAN: I wanted to see Mom.

IRIS: Won't do you any good.

FRAN: What do you mean?

IRIS: Won't recognize you. The only person she recognizes now is me, and that's only about half the time.

FRAN: What?

IRIS: I had to put her in a home nine months ago. Alzheimer's.

FRAN: Oh my lord.

IRIS: Sorry.

FRAN: When were you going to tell me!? After her funeral? Or never? She's my mother too you know.

IRIS: She wouldn't know that by the way you've stayed in touch.

FRAN: You made it very clear that I wasn't welcome in Seattle.

IRIS: Doesn't mean you couldn't have written her or called her, just once in a while. You know, letting her know you were okay.

FRAN: And would Mom and you have believed me?

*(FRAN takes envelope from her purse and gives it to IRIS.)*

IRIS: What's this?

FRAN: I wanted to give it to Mom.

IRIS: What is it?

FRAN: It's the three hundred and twenty dollars I stole from Mom's dresser when I ran away. I don't know if Mom even knew what happened to it.

IRIS: *(returns envelope to FRAN)* Mom can't count to five so keep it. *(softening)* Mom and I knew you took that money. Even if it meant we had to eat more macaroni and cheese we were glad you took it.

FRAN: You were?

IRIS: The only thing worse than imagining you in New York at eighteen was for you to be broke in New York at eighteen.

FRAN: I won't tell you how I spent it. That was a fortune for Mom then.

*(Beat.)*

IRIS: Did Lew call you?

FRAN: About what?

IRIS: You know about what. About this. *(gestures, indicating her condition)*

FRAN: No. I haven't heard from anyone in Seattle.

IRIS: So it's pure coincidence that you show up when I'm going out the door?

FRAN: I've been wanting to see you and Mom for a couple of years now and I had some free time this month. Airfares are low. I say to myself, Why not? I thought we might try, we might find a way, to patch things up. Sounds like it's too late, for Mom now. Great timing, huh?

IRIS: 'Fraid so. You've kept your figure.

FRAN: Well -

IRIS: Not everyone does that.

FRAN: Judging by that picture, you kept yours too. *(pause)* Did Mom ever get a headstone for Dad's grave?

IRIS: No, it would have been a waste of granite.

FRAN: You still feel that way?

IRIS: And you don't? So what is going on there in Baltimore? You're still there, right?

FRAN: Yes, still there.

IRIS: They have those crabs. The ones that you eat the shell and everything, right?

FRAN: Uh-huh, soft-shelled.

IRIS: That's right, soft-shelled. Do you like them?

FRAN: No, not particularly. What do you mean "going on"?

IRIS: You know what I mean. Your life. You have a life there, yes?

FRAN: Yes. Sort of. Actually I'm a special ed teacher in middle school.

IRIS: Really? Don't you have to go to college to do that?

FRAN: Yes, that's right, you do.

IRIS: Oh. Is there a husband? Or a guy?

FRAN: No.

IRIS:  No?

FRAN:  Well, a boyfriend, sort of, name's Mark.

IRIS:  Serious.

FRAN:  I don't know. Not too, I guess. Judging by the marriages of some of the other teachers, I probably shouldn't complain.

IRIS:  So no kids?

FRAN:  Hardly.

IRIS:  I can tell you it's not as if you've missed years of unqualifed joy.

FRAN:  Well I haven't had the chance to find that out.  And it's getting too late now. *(pause)* You and Lew.  No more children?

IRIS:  We tried.

FRAN:  *(with slightest hint of superiority)* Oh. *(pause)* Did Margaret ever want a brother or sister?

IRIS:  Maybe when she was younger, a little bit anyway.  As it turns out she's more than enough for one family.

FRAN:  *(examines family photo)* How is Margaret?

IRIS:  Her name's Meg.

FRAN:  She's so pretty and all grown up.  Has the Ross family nose doesn't she?

IRIS:  Took the photo in black and white so you couldn't see the purple in her hair.  She's a handful.

FRAN:  In what way a handful?

IRIS: When she's not busy rebelling she's setting new records for melancholy. On top of that she not only discovered the missing link between thug and brute, but she convinced herself that she's in love with it.

FRAN: Why does that sound familiar? What are her plans for the future?

IRIS: Mention the future and Meg thinks you mean tomorrow. Forget it.

FRAN: And how is Mom's drinking?

IRIS: That's how we discovered the Alzheimer's. When she laid off the bourbon I knew something was seriously wrong.

FRAN: She couldn't remember that she needed a drink?

IRIS: Or where she stashed the bottles. I don't know. The doctors say it happens sometime.

FRAN: I haven't had a drink in twelve years.

*(DIDGE enters, disheveled, wearing rubber boots.)*

IRIS: Didge, my sister Fran. Didge is our next door neighbor. She's like part of the family. Aren't you Didge?

DIDGE: Yes, I'm right next door, that's where I am. Been there for fifteen years. Preston and I. Well not fifteen years for Preston. He was my husband. He was next door for more like thirteen years. See, he passed -

IRIS: Did Lew find you?

DIDGE: You're the sister in Boston?

FRAN: Baltimore.

DIDGE: That's right. I knew it was a B.

FRAN: Her one and only sister.

IRIS: She's been gone a long time.

DIDGE: Well, welcome. Kind of a tough time for a visit, isn't it?

FRAN: Yeah, kinda.

DIDGE: *(to IRIS)* Does Lew have one of those Shopvac things?

IRIS: Yes, he has one. You didn't see him? He went looking for you. Something about crossed wires.

DIDGE: Oh, yeah, that's still a problem. No. I've just discovered water all over my basement from the kitchen pipes. Do you think I could borrow it, that Shopvac thing? I know they vacuum up things like leaves but I think they do water too. Isn't that right? Oh my lord, what a mess.

IRIS: Find Lew. He'll get it for you.

DIDGE: Thanks. Gotta run before the chimney collapses or the ceiling falls in or the front door comes off. Welcome again. From Baltimore. Hope to talk to you later.

FRAN: Thanks. Me too.

*(DIDGE exits.)*

FRAN: Whooo.

IRIS: Right. She's having her kitchen remodeled but I guess it's turned into a war zone.

FRAN: I want to see Mom, even if she doesn't know who I am.

IRIS: Be my guest.

FRAN: How long does she have?

IRIS: Four months at the outside. That's what they said last month anyway. So three months now. Maybe. I've learned that these doctors are too optimistic.

Who would have thought Mom would outlive me? Does bourbon work as a preservative?

FRAN: Didn't for me.

IRIS: Maybe I should have been entering bars instead of marathons.

FRAN: Well, apparently it didn't preserve her brain too well.

IRIS: Pickled it, more likely.

FRAN: How long? You know -

IRIS: A week, maybe.

FRAN: I'm sorry.

IRIS: That's the way it is kid. Mom is at Saint Olaf's Nursing Home. Lew can call you a taxi if you want to see her.

FRAN: Well, okay. . . . You know school, in Baltimore, doesn't start for three more weeks. I could maybe stay and help out a little, if you -

IRIS: No, not necessary. Between hospice, Lew and Didge, we've got things covered. You should probably see Mom and then go home.

FRAN: This is so ridiculous and idiotic and just plain, just plain fucked up. That's what it is.

IRIS: You're swearing again.

FRAN: I never stopped. Can't we just bury the hatchet, before we're buried?

IRIS: Cremated. I've specified cremated. It's all in that Notebook *(gestures)* I made for Lew.

FRAN: Too many years have gone by. I can't even remember what the hatchets were.

IRIS: Yes you can. There were lots and lots of hatchets. With different handles and sharp edges. I still have that letter you wrote after Meg and I came home from the hospital. I keep it quarantined in a glass jar.

FRAN: Oh, forgot about that. I was furious and I'm sure drunk. Can't even remember what I said. I'm sure I don't want to. After you left I felt like the world's biggest failure and went on a binge. But haven't enough years gone by -

IRIS: Actions always have consequences.

FRAN: Hasn't a high enough price been paid?

IRIS: I'm an attorney, not an accountant. By the time you were twenty you had caused enough grief for three lifetimes. You've always been out of control.

FRAN: Out of control then, out of control now, out of control forever. Is that the script?

IRIS: I didn't write it.

FRAN: How tragic that we can't all be in complete control like Saint Iris.

IRIS: You have your life in Baltimore and we have ours in Seattle.

FRAN: But this makes no fucking sense at all. You're not going to have a life in a few days.

IRIS: I don't need you to tell me.

(LEW enters.)

LEW: I had to get the Shopvac for Didge.

IRIS: We know. Now it's her basement.

LEW: Armageddon has struck over there.

IRIS: Over there?

FRAN: We know.

*(MEG enters, in pain, which she tries to hide.)*

MEG: Hi Mom. *(notices FRAN but doesn't recognize her)* Hi everyone.

IRIS: Meg, this is your Aunt Francine.

MEG: Hi. Yeah, hi. Wow. This is a surprise. I didn't know you were coming.

FRAN: Don't feel bad. Neither did they.

MEG: Oh, I see, I guess. Mom's told me a little about you.

FRAN: Why do I not want to hear it?

MEG: It wasn't that bad.

FRAN: You're such a big girl now.

MEG: I guess, yeah, sort of anyway. Those two still think I'm little.

LEW: Do not. We wish she was still our little girl.

MEG: *(to IRIS)* How's the pain?

*(IRIS looks away.)*

MEG: You look better than last night.

IRIS: I have no vanity left, but thank you anyway. You don't exactly look on top of the world yourself. *(notices Meg wincing)* What's wrong?

MEG: Nothing. I'm okay. Didn't sleep good is all. I need, I'd like to borrow the car, for an hour or two, no more than that.

LEW: Where are you going?

MEG: Out.

LEW:  That tells us a lot.

MEG:  I need to go to the store and get some things.

LEW:  Some things like what?

MEG:  Dad!  Girl, female things.

LEW:  You're going down to the jail, aren't you?

IRIS:  Jail?  Who's going to jail?

MEG:  *(to LEW)* Please, that's the last place I'd go!

LEW:  *(to IRIS)* Pete, for one.  He's already there. *(to MEG)* And that's where you're going to end up if you don't get rid of that boy.

IRIS:  What's this jail stuff?  And your Dad is right.

MEG:  Great.  This is just fucking great.

IRIS:  You don't need to swear Margaret.

FRAN:  I thought it was Meg.

LEW:  Great what?

IRIS:  *(to FRAN)* You stay out of this.

MEG:  *(to LEW)* You and Mom, you two pick a great time to finally agree on something.

LEW:  *(to IRIS)* I don't think that was a compliment.

MEG:  I'm done with that creep.

IRIS:  We've heard that before.

MEG: Well I am this time. Will you give me some credit? Quit being my parole officer and try being a mother!

IRIS: Parole officer is it?! So that's the gratitude I get! Parole officer! Thanks a million Meg.

MEG: And now you want to send me to jail in Montana.

IRIS: It's one of the finest schools in the country -

MEG: For what? Wigged out kids, right? Girls who gaze too fondly at the medicine cabinet? Boys who want to practice with their dad's shotgun? I'm not stupid. I know what you're doing.

LEW: Don't talk to your mother that way, young lady.

IRIS: *(to FRAN)* See what you've missed by not having kids?

LEW: It is a good school.

MEG: Sure it is. You don't know anything about it. You've just read what's in that Notebook. You're just saying that because she does. *(exhibits pain)* Look, I really need to borrow the car. And I swear to you I'm not going to jail.

IRIS: Why can't you tell us where you're going?

MEG: Because I just can't. Will you please trust me for once?

LEW: We have trusted you.

IRIS: And look where it got us.

MEG: I need you to trust me now.

LEW: If you can't tell us where you're going, you can't have the car.

IRIS: That's not being unreasonable.

*(MEG, grabbing her stomach, begins to cry. MEG runs off to bathroom. FRAN is shocked by what she is seeing.)*

FRAN: Isn't anyone going to help that poor girl!? I don't believe what I'm seeing.

*(FRAN exits to bathroom to check on Meg.)*

IRIS: Jail? What -

LEW: Pete was arrested on a DUI two nights ago. Wrecked his car. That's how Meg got banged up. I didn't want to worry you.

IRIS: This is what you get.

LEW: This is what you get what?

IRIS: Always, always, always you let her have her own way. Whenever I try to make her toe the line it's always "Poor Meg. Go easy on her. She's just a girl."

LEW: But you never would let us take it easy, would you? You always had to ride her hard, make her feel like a failure whenever she made a little mistake.

IRIS: Little mistake? Like sneaking off with a boy who wrecks a car and almost kills her.

LEW: It didn't almost kill her.

IRIS: How do you know? Were you there? Did you see the car? How do you even know how bad she was hurt?

LEW: Look, all I'm saying is, a little less judging and a little more affection could go a long way.

IRIS: So now I'm getting it from you too! What have I even lived here for? What have I been doing all that girl's life? Why have I even tried? You tell me! This is a fine way to say goodbye! Thanks one fucking lot Lew!

LEW: Your new vocabulary.

IRIS:  I know exactly what I'm saying!

LEW:  Honey, I didn't -

*(FRAN enters upset.)*

FRAN:  This isn't probably the best timing, but your daughter -

IRIS:  My daughter what?

FRAN:  Your daughter, well, she's having a miscarriage.  She -

IRIS:  Miscarriage!  That's not possible.  No, it can't be!  Oh my god!

FRAN:  I need to get her –

IRIS:  Miscarriage?  How do you know?

FRAN:  Trust me on this one, Sis.

IRIS:  But -

FRAN:  Personal experience.  Give me the car keys.  I'll take -

IRIS:  Lew, go get Didge!  She can take her.

FRAN:  I can take her.  I've been through this, okay?

IRIS:  Didge knows where the hospital is.

FRAN:  So does Meg.  It's not like she's unconscious.  She can give me directions.

*(LEW reaches into his pocket to give FRAN car keys.)*

IRIS:  *(to LEW)* Don't you do that!

FRAN:  I'll take her.

IRIS:  *(to FRAN)* Over my dead body!  *(to LEW)* Go get Didge.

LEW:  But -

IRIS:  *(to LEW)* But what? I suppose this is all my fault too. I'm the one who got her pregnant, right?

LEW:  I didn't -

FRAN:  Knock it off, both of you! I'm taking her to the hospital, and right now! You got that?! Give me the goddam keys!

IRIS:  You have no clue what Meg needs.

FRAN:  I sure as hell know what she needs right now: a doctor and fast.

IRIS:  You don't. No you don't, sister. Not a clue. You couldn't take care of any-one seventeen years ago and you don't know how to take care of her now!

*(IRIS collapses. LEW rushes to IRIS. FRAN stunned and hurt. LEW tosses keys to FRAN.)*

(INTERMISSION)

# ACT 2

## SCENE 1

*(Late that afternoon, Friday.  IRIS in wheelchair, still distraught over the morning's events.  DIDGE attempts to feed IRIS applesauce.)*

IRIS:  No, I can't eat anything.

DIDGE:  Now you tell me, when was the last time you ate?

IRIS:  I had some crackers.

DIDGE:  When?

IRIS:  Today.

DIDGE:  When today?

IRIS:  Before all hell broke loose.

DIDGE:  Iris, that's no good.

IRIS:  No good?!  It's been a complete disaster!

DIDGE:  I mean not eating.

IRIS:  I had some Seven-Up.

DIDGE:  Seven-Up doesn't count.  Here. *(moves a spoon of applesauce toward her mouth)*

IRIS:  No, I told you.  Get it away.

DIDGE: *(takes a little taste from the spoon)* Mmm, I'm telling you it's good.  I made it myself, from the first ripe apples off the Malus tree in my garden.

IRIS: What tree?

DIDGE: Never mind. Your husband was giving me a biology lesson.

IRIS: Those biology lessons can get you in trouble.

DIDGE: Maybe I should have put a little more sugar in it.

IRIS: I wouldn't know. All these drugs have my taste buds screwed up.

DIDGE: Any word from the hospital?

IRIS: Fran called a little while ago. The doctors say Meg's going to be okay.

DIDGE: Oh that's a relief.

IRIS: I'm not sure what okay means but yes it is. Jeez, can you imagine a baby around here? That's all Meg and Lew would need, another generation of trouble.

DIDGE: Somebody would need a mother then.

IRIS: All three.

DIDGE: Don't you think sometimes things really do work out for the best?

IRIS: *(looks at DIDGE skeptically, then glances at joints)* Have you been smoking one of those?

DIDGE: Is that what they really are?

IRIS: A present from Pete.

DIDGE: Never touched the stuff. You think Lew's okay?

IRIS: No. But at least he doesn't have to worry about being a grandfather.

DIDGE: For now anyway. I just remember what a tough time I had when I lost Preston. I don't think Lew's eating hardly at all.

IRIS: Wish I could say that about his drinking.

DIDGE: Both of you are going to end up skeletons.

*(IRIS looks at DIDGE sharply.)*

DIDGE: Oh, I'm sorry. What a stupid -

IRIS: Forget about it.

DIDGE: I made him a chicken salad sandwich.

IRIS: He loves those.

DIDGE: I know. But it's still sitting in the fridge. I think he forgot it was there.

IRIS: Probably did. It's always been a mystery how he can be the world's leading expert on Douglas fir trees but can't find his razor in the morning.

DIDGE: Can't find his razor for the trees.

IRIS: Does he look that bad to you too?

DIDGE: Like someone who sees a tree falling on him but can't get his feet to move.

IRIS: What kind of tree?

DIDGE: A giant one. The kind that when it falls, it shakes the ground with a boom you can hear half a mile away. That kind.

IRIS: I'm doing my best to get him ready. To get both of them ready.

*(Honk-cries of blue herons are heard. IRIS looks up out the window.)*

IRIS: There go the herons headed down to the canal.

DIDGE: Dinner time.

IRIS: Swimming somewhere in that canal is a salmon who has no clue that his life is going to end in a few minutes.

(*More heron honk-cries, but fainter now.*)

DIDGE: Some of those salmon have swum here all the way from Russia.

IRIS: Doesn't matter. For one of them the journey's about to end in the beak of a blue heron. Didge, did you ever feel that your mother was too tough on you?

DIDGE: Not near as tough as that heron's going to be on a salmon.

IRIS: Didge?

DIDGE: All girls feel that way sometimes. Look, I think you've been a terrific mother. It's not like kids don't need boundaries.

IRIS: Listening to them you'd think I put up twelve-foot high concrete barriers with barbed wire.

DIDGE: There's more things under this roof than one person can worry about.

IRIS: (*trying to lighten conversation*) Does your house still have its roof?

DIDGE: (*smiling*) It did an hour ago. (*again offers IRIS a spoon of applesauce*) Here.

IRIS: No, I can't.

DIDGE: Come on, just taste it.

IRIS: (*tentatively tastes, then accepts the spoon*) What'd you call it?

DIDGE: Malus sauce. From my -

IRIS: It's not bad. Thanks. Do you think things could become any bigger of a mess around here?

*(DIDGE gives IRIS a few more spoonfuls. FRAN and MEG enter, returning from hospital. Other than looking washed out, MEG appears all right. When IRIS sees FRAN and MEG she declines any more applesauce. FRAN and MEG behave gingerly around IRIS.)*

IRIS: *(to DIDGE)* That's enough. I can't eat anymore. *(to MEG)* Hi Meg.

MEG: Hi Mom. What you having?

DIDGE: Homemade applesauce. Want some?

MEG: You made it?

DIDGE: Uh-huh.

MEG: No, I'm not hungry.

FRAN: Didn't the doctor say you should eat something light when you got home, and then go to bed?

MEG: Oh, right.

DIDGE: There's more in the fridge.

FRAN: Why don't you eat some? Then get to bed.

MEG: Okay.

*(IRIS is amazed at MEG's compliance.)*

DIDGE: *(to IRIS)* If you're done with this -

IRIS: I'm done.

DIDGE: Then I'll take it in and dish some out for Meg.

IRIS: *(to DIDGE)* Okay. Thanks.

*(MEG, unsure, goes to give IRIS a hug. They hug, tentatively, then with feeling.)*

IRIS: I'm glad you're okay. I'm sorry about -

MEG: It's okay. I'm sorry too.

*(MEG and DIDGE begin to exit toward kitchen.)*

FRAN: *(to MEG)*
I'll come and check on you in a little bit. Remember you're supposed to keep your legs elevated.

MEG: Okay.

*(MEG and DIDGE exit.)*

IRIS: She looks better than I expected. How is she?

FRAN: I think she's fine. Well, hardly fine, but I think, the doctors think, she'll be okay. The emotional part is probably worse than the physical stuff.

IRIS: Personal experience?

FRAN: Hmm.

IRIS: Did the doctors say anything, you know, about long-term damage?

FRAN: No, as far as they can tell, she'll be able to have children. The E.R. doctor, who didn't look much older than Meg, told her she needed to take it easy for a couple of weeks.

IRIS: What did Meg say?

FRAN: She kind of nodded.

IRIS: Nodding is the height of agreement for that girl.

FRAN: On your back, being poked, with your feet in stirrups, is not a girl's best fighting position.

IRIS: Meg's able to fight from any position. *(pause)* So now I guess we have two invalids in the house.

FRAN: I wouldn't exactly call her an invalid. . . . Look, about this morning -

IRIS: Forget it.

FRAN: I don't think we can do that Iris.

IRIS: You didn't forget we have an agreement.

FRAN: No I didn't, counsellor.

IRIS: Did you tell her -

FRAN: What I told her was that if she got pregnant again before she was twenty-five and married I would personally string her up.

IRIS: You know -

FRAN: I know.

IRIS: Meg knows nothing. I want it to stay that way.

FRAN: I've honored that agreement for seventeen years; don't worry.


## ACT 2, SCENE 2

*(Monday morning, three days later. IRIS alone, in bed, depressed, distraught, at the end of her rope. It's clear that IRIS's health has continued to deteriorate. IRIS looks at the third gift, opens it. It's a small book of inspirational poetry, the last thing she wants to see; tosses it across the room. Sees the box containing the joints. Ponders. Decides "What the hell." Lights one, smokes it. FRAN enters, shocked to see IRIS smoking pot.)*

IRIS: Hey, it's been twenty-five years.

FRAN: I don't believe what I'm seeing.

IRIS: What are they going to do, put me in jail with Pete?

*(IRIS offers FRAN a toke. FRAN declines. IRIS stubs out the joint.)*

IRIS: That's probably enough. I don't know how well it mixes with the morphine.

FRAN: Opiates and cannabis, the good old days. Sort of anyway.

IRIS: If I had known morphine was this good I would have grown more poppies.

FRAN: *(looks at the remaining joints)* Where'd you get them?

IRIS: The Burpee catalog.

FRAN: The pot, where'd you get the pot?

IRIS: Pete is not completely devoid of skills. He deals drugs.

FRAN: Oh that's useful.

IRIS: If it'll keep him in jail and away from her it's useful. I don't want you to tell Meg.

FRAN: I already told you -

IRIS: *(points to the extinguished joint)* No, about this.

FRAN: My god Iris, do you really think Meg's been living in a convent? You got it from her boyfriend, right?

IRIS: Oh, you're right. Well flush this down the toilet.

FRAN: She's going to smell it. Probably already does.

IRIS: Then open that window.

*(FRAN opens window, exits to flush joint down toilet. IRIS hides remaining joints and waves at the air. FRAN quickly returns.)*

FRAN: *(looking outside)* Your garden is beautiful. Like in a magazine.

IRIS: That's one of the main reasons I wanted to come home, to be here when . . .

FRAN: I like to garden but I only have a postage stamp of a yard.

IRIS: You garden?

FRAN: You've got blackspot on your roses.

IRIS: I know. If you look closely you can see signs of winter coming. The roses are slowing down, this is probably their last flush. The dogwood leaves are show-ing some yellow.

FRAN: I see that.

IRIS: When does your flight leave?

FRAN: Tomorrow afternoon. That's the schedule. I didn't know how long -

IRIS: Of course. No one does. What are you going to do in Baltimore?

FRAN: Well I've got a school district conference to attend next week. Then I'll resume my little life; get ready for the school year.

IRIS: This special ed stuff -

FRAN: It's called teaching. That "stuff" is teaching.

IRIS: It probably means a lot to your students. And their families. I would imag-ine it means a lot. Particularly for those students . . . who are special.

*(Beat.)*

FRAN: Do you know, I believe that is the first time in my life my sister has given me a compliment.

IRIS: No it's not.

FRAN: Yes it is.

IRIS: No it's not.

FRAN: Yes it is.

IRIS: Oh come on, that can't be true.

FRAN: Nothing I ever did was as good as you. And you and Mom made sure I knew it.

IRIS: Drugs distorted your memory.

FRAN: You set the bar so high I would have needed a pole vault to get over it.

IRIS: You are wrong about this.

FRAN: Oh am I? You had to have the nicer clothes, the cuter boyfriends, the higher grades. You even had to win the boob contest, making sure I knew yours were bigger.

IRIS: I really did that?

FRAN: Yes you really did that!

IRIS: And I guess I've won the race to the finish line too. Welcome to my victory party.

FRAN: It's not like I was invited.

IRIS: I know, you've been to one of those therapists who plant memories in your head for you to blame things on so you don't have to take responsibility.

FRAN: Right. That's where I've been. It didn't take a therapist to see your shadow, hovering like some cobra over a mouse.

IRIS: Hardly a mouse. Not you. For god's sake Mom was a basketcase. We were both kids. Heck, with the shape Mom was in, we were like three kids. I did the best I knew how.

FRAN: Your best was always making me feel like shit! Your best has been shutting me out of your and Mom's and Meg's life for the last seventeen years.

IRIS: I didn't make you run away and screw up your life. You're the one who got pregnant. You shut yourself out of Meg's life by being in no condition to raise a child! You can't hang any of that on me!

FRAN: Who else was I supposed to call?

IRIS: I don't know.

FRAN: There wasn't anyone else.

IRIS: I wonder why not.

FRAN: Just my tyrant sister in Seattle.

IRIS: Tyrant, is that an upgrade from cobra?

FRAN: You always made yourself Miss Biggie by stepping on me.

IRIS: You really could have left your claws in Baltimore.

FRAN: Then stop snarling!

IRIS: You're the one snarling!

(Pause to catch their breath.)

IRIS: We both had claws. They helped us survive. And mine weren't really bigger than yours.

FRAN: What?

IRIS: I just bought bigger bras and lied. Let's call it a tie. (looks down at her own chest) In fact right now you're winning. . . . Are you going to come back for Mom's funeral?

FRAN: That a warning or a request? As you've said, Mom won't care.

IRIS: Maybe your boyfriend, what's his name?

FRAN: Mark.

IRIS: Maybe Mark could come back with you.

FRAN: *(hesitates)* I don't know. There's also Tony.

IRIS: You have two boyfriends?

FRAN: No.

IRIS: How many are there?

FRAN: Tony's not my boyfriend. He's Mark's.

IRIS: Oh. But you said -

FRAN: He is my best friend, but . . . Mark's terrific and we get along lots better than he does with Tony, but some things just can't . . .

IRIS: Somebody's going to have to make Mom's arrangements. I'm not going to be here. And Lew . . . Maybe this Mark would still come back with you, for Mom's funeral. Maybe his Tony could come too.

FRAN: I don't think so.

IRIS: What I feel worst about . . .

FRAN: There's a lot to pick from. We have shit all over our past.

IRIS: Not the past. Not that it was so great. The future. I'm not going to be around for Meg's life, the rest of it: her beaus, her broken hearts, her wedding - singular I hope - her children, my grandchildren. *(pause)* Meg has always been more like you. Didn't matter what Lew or I did, that's just who she was. Now she's at this difficult age -

FRAN: Tell me about it.

IRIS: She doesn't listen to me, not anymore. But with you -

FRAN: It's because I'm not her mother. Her age requires no more logic than that.

IRIS: God knows I haven't been much use to her this past year. Maybe she'd continue to listen to you.

FRAN: Whoa there, I've barely been here forty-eight hours and I'm leaving tomorrow.

IRIS: Your departure.

FRAN: Yes?

IRIS: Do you think it could be delayed for a day or two?

FRAN: God I don't know Iris.

IRIS: Until my departure.

*(FRAN remains silent.)*

IRIS: You already said that maybe you could stay a few days.

FRAN: And you already informed me that I needed to leave.

IRIS: Couldn't you at least call the airline?

*(FRAN does not reply.)*

IRIS: Look, I know this is probably out of the question, with your job in Baltimore and all the foul water under the rusty Seattle bridge, but do you think you might even consider staying for longer than a few days?

FRAN: If you're going where I think you're going, don't do this.

IRIS: Where am I going?

FRAN: I don't even want to guess.

IRIS: Why not?

FRAN: Why not! Don't, Iris.

IRIS: I think I need to.

*(Beat.)*

FRAN: Like how much longer?

IRIS: I don't know. Well, could you, do you think? Have you ever thought about coming back home . . . you know, for good?

*(FRAN is pierced by words "coming back home," starts to cry, then sadness and anger rise.)*

FRAN: Do you know what you're saying?

IRIS: I'm not sure.

FRAN: How strong was that dope? You never wanted me around.

IRIS: That's not true. Mom and I were shattered when you ran away.

FRAN: I mean after that. You never wanted me around.

IRIS: Can't you understand why Lew and I wouldn't have, after Meg came along, the shape you were in?

FRAN: I can't do this.

IRIS: Why not? Going to run away again?

FRAN: Don't start that. I am not the one who's running away this time.

IRIS: Are you suggesting -

FRAN: I'm not suggesting anything. Now that you might need someone here, you think I can just turn my back on my life in Baltimore and come hightailing it back.

IRIS: It's not me that needs you. I'm going to be gone in a few days.

FRAN: I have a life that I've carefully built for myself a long way from here.

IRIS: Living alone, with a gay boyfriend.

FRAN: With my life intact. Sober. A career. Anyway I've already signed a teaching contract for next year.

IRIS: I know a good attorney. In fact, there are about thirty of them in my firm who would help you out - pro bono.

FRAN: You've always made it very clear that I'm a fuck-up and not wanted here.

IRIS: I did what I thought was best, for Meg's sake.

FRAN: Before Meg.

IRIS: Maybe back then . . . I don't know. I'm in no position to lie here and plead innocent.

FRAN: Iris Ross, my esteemed sister, not always right?

IRIS: It's possible.

FRAN: Haven't seen this before.

IRIS: Well it can happen. Not often, though. What do I need to do - get down on my knees, say I'm sorry and beg? I'm thinking maybe you can be good for Meg. You're a veteran of these skirmishes, right? Show her your scars. Don't think of it as permanent. See Meg and Lew through this rough patch and then go back to Baltimore if that's what you really want.

FRAN: Meg and Lew?

IRIS: Well he lives here too. He is her father.

FRAN: Have you talked to Lew about this?

IRIS: No.

FRAN: What would he think?

IRIS: Lew's not being terribly cooperative about my plans for his future. This one's not in that Notebook.

FRAN: So what do you think, that he would think?

IRIS: He'd probably be all right with it. He's the one who called you, isn't he?

FRAN: Well . . .

IRIS: If you lie to someone on their deathbed, they come back to haunt you.

FRAN: Is that right?

IRIS: I don't know. But if they can, I will. I think he'd be pleased. And plus you could help him with the Didge situation.

FRAN: I'm no good at remodelling.

IRIS: No, a Didge romance situation.

FRAN: Oh.

IRIS: For some reason Lew is worried that Didge has romantic designs on him.

FRAN: Does she?

IRIS: Maybe a little. Nothing too serious. Since I came home from the hospital, I've been having - well, she's a real sweetheart - but I've been having a hard time imagining them together.

FRAN: I've seen stranger pairs. What's wrong with Didge?

IRIS: Nothing's wrong with Didge. She's a great person who really cares about Meg and Lew. It's just in that way . . . I don't think so.

FRAN: Who ever knows how things turn out?

IRIS: I used to think I could arrange the world, so as to reduce the casualties. Hmff. The gods laugh at us.

FRAN: If I come back, and I'm not saying I would, the only reason, it'd be for Meg. I don't even want to think about going down any road with Lew.

IRIS: What any road?

FRAN: You know what road.

IRIS: He'd be relieved to know that. It's just that you'd be a big help with Meg plus you'd give him a Didge buffer. . . . When Meg was little we'd sit here at night and I'd explain that each star is a sun shining on gardens far, far away and then we'd make up stories about the strange plants that grow there. Look, I've poured my life into your creation and now it's your turn.

FRAN: You're her mother.

IRIS: Not for much longer.

FRAN: No, forever.

IRIS: No forever. Meg's going to need you.

FRAN: That must have been some dope you were smoking. I don't think so Iris. A daughter? Overnight? A widowed brother-in-law for a roommate? What's wrong with this picture?

IRIS: At least stay for a couple of days.

FRAN: I don't know.

IRIS: Call the airline to see if an extension is possible.

FRAN: Back off, okay? I just don't know.

IRIS: Don't say no yet.

## ACT 2, SCENE 3

*(A few hours later, Monday morning. IRIS in deep sleep. FRAN observes IRIS. LEW has been studying Notebook and is now holding it. MEG enters in bathrobe.)*

MEG:  Mom looks completely out.

LEW:  Dead asleep. Finally took some morphine, thank goodness.

MEG:  She's going downhill fast, isn't she?

*(LEW and FRAN do not respond.)*

MEG:  *(smells residual pot odor)* It smells funny in here. What is that?

FRAN:  I think some of your mother's medicine is causing bad gas.

MEG:  *(quizzical)* That's not what it smells like. *(thinks, while she looks at IRIS)* No, no way, not in a million years, not Mom.

FRAN:  I'm starved.

*(MEG now looks at FRAN with suspicion.)*

FRAN:  Hey, don't look at me, I haven't had anything to eat yet this morning.

*(FRAN exits. LEW sees that IRIS has had an accident in bed. LEW feels like this is the last straw. MEG sees LEW's distress.)*

MEG:  What's wrong?

LEW:  Your mother had an accident.

MEG:  Where's the nurse?

LEW:  She started to give your mother a bath this morning.

MEG:  So where is she now?

LEW:  She walked out.

MEG:  Nurses aren't supposed to walk out.

LEW:  Your mother's pain was real bad.  This nurse had been up with another patient all night and when your mom started barking, she just upped and walked out.

MEG:  I kinda know how the nurse felt.

LEW:  The hospice people are supposed to send another one over.

MEG:  They should realize that people like in Mom's condition probably aren't going to be in the world's greatest mood.

LEW:  *(surprised at Meg's mature observation and defense of Iris)* You would think so, wouldn't you?  You still need a nurse yourself.

MEG:  No I don't.  I'm okay.  Really, I am.  The Ross girls are tough stock. *(with some hesitation)* Maybe I could . . .

LEW:  Do you think?

MEG:  I guess.  I mean, she's cleaned plenty of my messes.

LEW:  *(distraught)* I don't know how much more of this —

MEG:  Dad, I'll take care of it.

*(LEW moves aside.  MEG places a towel over the accident site.  When MEG raises IRIS's nightgown, MEG is shocked.  LEW notices.)*

LEW:  What is it?

MEG:  I didn't know.  I guess I just never thought about it.

LEW:  What?

MEG:  The hair.  Down there.  Ugh!

LEW: You lose it all over. I should have warned you.

MEG: No it's okay.

*(IRIS is semi-conscious. MEG decides to give IRIS a bed bath. Makes preparations. First cleans IRIS's face with damp washrag. MEG exhibits affection and sadness. MEG continues with bath, cleaning IRIS around her bottom. FRAN enters, eating a piece of toast. MEG exhibits confusion and alarm.)*

MEG: Aunt Fran -

FRAN: Do you need a hand?

MEG: No. Do you know what a C-section looks like, I mean a scar from one?

FRAN: *(without thinking)* Well the way they do them anymore you can't see it.

MEG: Why?

FRAN: Because your hair hides it.

MEG: Could you come over here?

*(FRAN is really confused. Lew gets "oh shit" look on his face. FRAN goes to MEG and IRIS.)*

MEG: Do you see a scar? Show me the scar.

FRAN: Well they fade over the years.

MEG: There's no scar.

*(FRAN tries to look away.)*

MEG: Look, please. Please look here! Do you see a scar?

FRAN: I don't know.

MEG: There is no scar!

*(FRAN examines IRIS.)*

FRAN:  No, no I can't see one.  Why is this -

MEG:  Because I was born by C-section.  What is going on?  Oh, my god!  Dad, what is going on here?

LEW:  What do you mean?

MEG:  You know what I mean?  Who had me?  Who is my mother?

LEW:  That woman there.

MEG:  Wasn't I born by C-section?

LEW:  Your mother loved you more than anyone or anything else in this world.

MEG:  I know, but who was my mother?

LEW:  Bearing a child is just biology's UPS truck.

MEG:  A truck?!

LEW:  Raising a child, that's the real labor and pain.

MEG:  I want to know whose womb I came out of.

LEW:  I can't tell.

MEG:  Why the hell not?

LEW:  I can't.  Shhh, you're going to wake your mother.

MEG:  My freakin' point.  Who is my mother?  And you.  For that matter, who are you?  Are you my father?  Who am I?

LEW:  I am the man who's been here all your life.

MEG:  Why can't you tell me?

LEW: I can't. Not now. Shh.

MEG: Why not?

LEW: I can't Meg. I promised your mother.

MEG: What mother was that?

LEW: You have to trust me.

MEG: I do not believe this! This is not happening. Do you know how completely fucking crazy this all is!?

## ACT 2, SCENE 4

*(Late that afternoon, Monday. IRIS is just waking up. LEW depressed and frazzled.)*

IRIS: How long was I asleep?

LEW: All afternoon. After the morphine you were out cold.

IRIS: I'm really thirsty. Would you get me some Seven-Up?

*(LEW brings glass of Seven-Up.)*

IRIS: What's this towel?

LEW: You had another accident.

IRIS: Do you know how tired I am of this degradation? How big a mess was it?

LEW: Wasn't much. Not much at all. Don't worry about it.

IRIS: When did the new nurse show up?

LEW: She didn't, hasn't, not yet anyway. We're still expecting one.

IRIS:  Then who helped, who did this?

LEW:  Your daughter.

IRIS:  You gotta be kidding.  Meg?

LEW:  No, I'm not kidding.

IRIS:  From patient to nurse, in what, three days?  That's a remarkable transformation.  Come over here, Mr. van Gogh.

LEW:  Mr. Who?

IRIS:  Let me look at your ear.

LEW:  Oh, that, it's fine now.  Haven't pruned it lately.

IRIS:  As long as you can still hear.

LEW:  *(joking; then serious)* What? . . . You had an accident while you were asleep, that's all.

IRIS:  I'm sorry.  It happened sometimes in the hospital too.  Meg really helped out?

LEW:  Uh-huh.  Really helped out.

IRIS:  The nurse can change the sheet later.

LEW:  Something else happened.

IRIS:  Didge's roof collapsed.

LEW:  No, not yet.  Not as far as I know.  Why didn't we ever tell Meg the truth?

IRIS:  What? You know why.  We didn't know if Fran - in fact all signs pointed the other way - was going to get her life squared away, was even going to live.  Meg didn't need to know what a screwed-up nest she fell out of.

LEW: I shouldn't have listened to you. I wanted to let her know as soon as she was old enough. Now I, I think we blew it.

IRIS: I don't need this Lew. Not now. We agreed together. All three of us. We all signed that agreement. What is this all about?

*(LEW is reluctant.)*

IRIS: Lew? Tell me now.

LEW: Meg has learned we're not her parents, you know, her birth parents.

IRIS: Goddam that Fran. We shouldn't have let her in -

LEW: It wasn't Fran.

IRIS: How else -

LEW: Meg saw -

IRIS: That agreement is in the safety deposit box.

LEW: Not the agreement.

IRIS: Saw what then?

LEW: That you didn't have a C-section.

IRIS: How would she know that? What has been going on?

LEW: After your little accident, Meg gave you a bath.

IRIS: Our Meg, gave me a bath?

LEW: Yes, she gave you a bath. All over. Like a nurse. Then she saw there was no C-section.

IRIS: We never told her about any C-section.

LEW: I did, once.

IRIS: How could you have been so careless?

LEW: Trying to be a father.

IRIS: Lew!

LEW: Forget that. It's done. The point is that there's a lot of crap crashing on top of her right now.

IRIS: On her! Where is she?

LEW: Upstairs asleep. I just looked in on her.

IRIS: So she doesn't know that Fran -

LEW: No. But now Meg's furious with you and me. She begged me to tell her.

IRIS: You didn't.

LEW: No, I told her I couldn't, I had made a promise. Fran's not in too great a mood either.

IRIS: Where's she?

LEW: Out for a walk. Needed some fresh air. I'm really worried about her.

IRIS: What's wrong with Fran?

LEW: Meg, not Fran. Come on.

IRIS: I have a plan.

LEW: Half of them backfire.

IRIS: Don't lay into me. Someone's had to do the planning.

LEW: Okay, let's hear it, your latest.

IRIS: Has Fran talked to you about her schedule, her travel schedule?

LEW: No.

IRIS: Fran has changed.

LEW: I know.

IRIS: You shouldn't have called her without talking to me first. But now that she's here I have to admit she's come a long ways. Remarkable actually. But what I really can't believe is how Meg listens to her, in a way she hasn't with us for years.

LEW: Kindred spirits.

IRIS: Maybe. . . I've asked Fran to stay.

LEW: You've what?

IRIS: You heard me.

LEW: *(sarcastic)* This is great.

IRIS: It might work.

LEW: And we tell Meg?

MEG: No, we tell Meg nothing. Not about that.

LEW: Then what do we tell her?

IRIS: We tell her she was adopted.

LEW: She's already figured that much out.

IRIS: Listen, will you? Tell her it was a society family who was afraid of a scandal, so they made us sign an agreement that Meg could never be told who her birth mother was until ten years after the woman's death.

LEW: And you think she'll buy that?

IRIS: It'll appeal to the drama queen in her. Those sort of agreements happen all the time. She'll buy it.

LEW: I don't think so. And Fran. Have you given her a Notebook?

IRIS: No.

LEW: When did you start arranging her life?

IRIS: What's today?

LEW: Monday.

IRIS: Then it was this morning. I'm pretty sure it was this morning.

LEW: Stay here? Fran?

IRIS: Yes, stay here, for a little while anyway.

LEW: How little is a while?

IRIS: A few days, maybe longer.

LEW: How much longer?

IRIS: Well, I've asked if she'd move back to Seattle, maybe for good.

LEW: Oh, that little while. No wonder she needed some air. And?

IRIS: She needed to think about it. You don't know if she called the airline?

LEW: I saw her on the phone. Don't know what about. Honey . . .

IRIS: Yes?

LEW: It's Meg. I don't know. I'm worried she could fall apart or . . .

IRIS: *(becoming tender)* I know. That's why I've asked Fran. You're not the only one who's scared. I'm the one losing my grip here. For me there's no bigger badder wolf in the whole forest.

*(Honk-cries of blue herons are heard. IRIS looks out the window.)*

LEW:  We never saw this coming.

IRIS:  Who ever does?

LEW:  I wish I could chop this goddam cancer down like a tree and burn it.  It's killing the most important person in my life. *(pause)* Lately I've been remembering . . .

IRIS:  What?

LEW:  The last time . . . we were together, that way.

IRIS:  What way?

LEW:  You know, that way.  It was last summer, that weekend at Mt. Rainier.  It's been a long time.

IRIS:  Don't get any ideas.  I've got a headache.

*(Both are amused.)*

IRIS:  That was a wonderful weekend.

LEW:  Little did we know the cancer was already inside you.

IRIS:  Remember all those wildflowers blooming their little heads off?

LEW:   And the marmots poking their heads out of their burrows, like furry periscopes.

IRIS:  I've gone back to that afternoon too.

LEW:  You have?

IRIS:  In the hospital.  I couldn't fill up all my time making plans.  Come over here.  At least we can hold each other.

*(LEW goes to bed; is tentative.)*

IRIS: It's all right. You can get in.

LEW: You're skin and bones. I'm worried that I'll crush you.

IRIS: We're both stronger than you think.

*(LEW gets onto bed, carefully. They hug.)*

LEW: When we were at Mt. Rainier, if we had known we could have made more of an occasion out of it.

IRIS: We never know when it's the last time. How would we have celebrated, if we had known?

LEW: I don't know. Candles. And sparklers we could have lit from the candles.

IRIS: Where would we have gotten sparklers?

LEW: Maybe left over from the Fourth of July. And we'd eat trail gorp.

IRIS: The kind with the M&Ms.

LEW: Chased down with ice cold champagne.

IRIS: Champagne gives me a headache.

LEW: Wrong time for a headache. Then that sparkling Italian wine you like.

IRIS: Moscato.

LEW: Yes, Moscato. But ice cold.

IRIS: Almost slush.

LEW: Bracing on the tongue. To help lock that afternoon in our memory. So we never forget.

## ACT 2, SCENE 5

*(Next evening, Tuesday. IRIS in bed, having recently expired. LEW on phone talking to funeral home. Notebook open on his lap.)*

LEW: So what time will you be by, to get her, my wife, her body I mean? . . . I see. It's 4329 McGraw, on Magnolia. . . That's 4329. . . Yes. Right next to the park . . . No, on the south side. . . That's right. No, she wants to be cremated. . . I see. . . Well, she's already filled that out. It's right here. . . Okay. . . That will be fine. What am I talking about? No, it won't be fine! Nothing is fine. . . Okay, okay, I'm all right.

*(FRAN enters upset. Waits for LEW to end call.)*

LEW: Should I do anything, with her, you know, until you come? . . . Within the hour? Okay. I'll wait by the door.
*(ends call; to FRAN)*
Meg took it pretty hard.

FRAN: Real hard.

LEW: Has she calmed down any?

FRAN: I can't tell.

LEW: If she's still hysterical, hugging her pillow, in the fetal position? That would be a clue.

FRAN: I can't tell.

LEW: Why not?

FRAN: Because Lew she's gone.

*(LEW, confused, looks toward Iris.)*

FRAN: Meg!

LEW: *(still confused)* Meg? Gone. She can't be gone.

FRAN: She's gone. I think she ran away.

LEW: Oh shit!

FRAN: I know.

LEW: I need to find her.

FRAN: I'm pretty sure I know where she is.

LEW: Where?

FRAN: At the train station. I'll go there now. You stay here, wait for the funeral home people. I need your keys.

LEW: Do you know where it is? *(gives her the keys)*

FRAN: Still at First and Jackson?

LEW: Hasn't moved.

FRAN: I can get there.

LEW: Should we call the police?

FRAN: Let's try this first.

LEW: You sure?

FRAN: I don't know. Jeez! I think so. If she's not there, then we'll call them.

*(FRAN dashes out. LEW looks after Fran, then looks at Iris.)*

## ACT 2, SCENE 6

*(Later that evening. MEG and FRAN on bench in train station.)*

MEG: How'd you find me?

FRAN: Next time you run away, probably shouldn't leave the train schedule up on your computer.

MEG: Oh. I'm not running away.

FRAN: What else do you call it? "Emigration" doesn't quite fit.

MEG: I never got a chance to ask her.

FRAN: Your Mom?

*(MEG nods.)*

FRAN: For what, permission to bail?

MEG: No, who my Mom really was. Dad won't tell me. Says she was just some UPS truck. Did she wear those brown shorts?

FRAN: Would knowing who bore you change anything about what Iris has done?

MEG: She should have told me. I have a right to know.

FRAN: Maybe. Maybe not. I'm sure she and Lew had good reasons.

MEG: Name one!

FRAN: Look, it didn't happen, okay. And now your Mom is gone. Your mother is the woman who fed and fretted and cleaned and coddled and cared for you, more than she did for anything else. I think you're too bright a girl to let this cancel out everything she and Lew, everything your parents have done for you all your life.

MEG: Why didn't she want me?

FRAN:  Iris did want you, more than anyone.

MEG:  No, my mother.

FRAN:  Wrong question.  Why were you so lucky to end up with Iris and Lew?  They devoted their lives to you?  Kids who aren't wanted get born every day.

MEG:  But why did she -

FRAN:  Tell me what you would have done if you hadn't  miscarried.

MEG:  I don't know.  I still had time to . . .

FRAN:  Are you really ready to spend the next twenty years raising a child?  Your mother was probably some scared kid a lot like you.

*(MEG doesn't respond.)*

FRAN:  Confusing, huh?

*(FRAN gives MEG envelope.)*

MEG:  What's this?

*(FRAN doesn't respond.  MEG opens envelope and counts the money.)*

MEG:  Three hundred and twenty dollars.  What is it?

FRAN:  Money I stole from your grandma twenty years ago.

MEG:  Why'd you do that?

FRAN:  To do the same thing you're doing.

MEG:  Emigrating?

FRAN:  Sitting alone - believe it or not – in this exact same train station, scared, running away, heading east.  I guess it's kind of hard to take a train out of Seattle heading west.

MEG: Were you talking to some weirdo aunt you'd never seen before?

FRAN: I brought the money as a peace offering but now that your grandma can't recognize Andrew Jackson, you might as well have it. It's not worth what it was in 1982 but it'll still buy a few meals.

*(MEG is thinking.)*

MEG: You took that train. Right? Doesn't look like it hurt you.

FRAN: You're looking at a retouched photo. You weren't there during the war.

MEG: War?

FRAN: With casualties. My problems just went along with me to New York.

MEG: Was there a Pete, you know, that you were dealing with?

FRAN: Not here, but I quickly found a couple of them in New York.

MEG: They want to send me away to some special school in Montana.

FRAN: Well, that would get you away from Pete.

MEG: I'm sure that was part of the plan.

FRAN: So is Montana where you're headed?

MEG: Going through Montana, not stopping there.

FRAN: It seems to me that what school you attend is now up to you and your Dad. Where are you going, after you go through Montana?

MEG: All the way to New York.

FRAN: Great choice for someone your age.

MEG: I know a girl whose father got transferred there last year. I can maybe stay with her.

FRAN:  Maybe?

MEG:  Probably.  It's been such a fucking circus here.  Mom went and got this cancer.  Dad's clueless half the time.  Of the three, Didge has been the rock if you can imagine that.

FRAN:  Iris didn't go and get this cancer.  Come on Meg.  Some day you'll appreciate everything she's done.

MEG:  You try and live with her.

FRAN:  I did.  Iris changed my diapers too.  She's not always easy but, come on, we're not really talking about the Wicked Witch of the West here.

*(MEG is unconvinced.)*

FRAN:  Your Mom pretty much raised me and took care of your grandma to boot. Iris was carrying a big load.

MEG:  She didn't have a parent dying.

FRAN:  What do you know about your grandfather?

MEG:  Your and Mom's dad?

FRAN:  The same.

MEG:  I don't know.  Mom said he was a no-good who ran out on you guys when you were little.

FRAN:  Not so little.  Your Mom was fourteen.

MEG:  I remember Mom telling me that when he left for California he had a big suitcase and was wearing a white shirt and a skinny brown tie.  Did you guys ever visit him there, like to go to Disneyland and stuff?

FRAN:  No.

MEG:  How come?

FRAN:  He was hard to get hold of.

MEG:  Did he like ever get married again?

FRAN:  Nope.

MEG:  Have you ever gone back to visit his grave?

FRAN:  Where's that?

MEG:  California, I guess.

FRAN:  He's not buried in California.

MEG:  Where then?

FRAN:  There's an unmarked grave somewhere in Seattle.  He never got to California.

MEG:  What do you mean?

FRAN:  He never left the garage.  That's where your Mom found him.  She first saw the kicked-over suitcase and then his legs and then -

MEG:  You mean -

FRAN:  I mean.

MEG:  I had no idea.  Mom never -

FRAN:  It's not something you want to talk about, now is it?  The years of security Iris gave you are a lot more than she ever got.  They're a bunch more than a lot of people get in this fucked-up world.

MEG:  Mom never swears.

FRAN:  Whereas I would have made one hell of a goddam good sailor, don't you think?

MEG: How do I even know who I am now?

FRAN: As I recall, that's part of being seventeen. It takes a lifetime.

MEG: Who was my mother?

FRAN: Maybe some day -

MEG: Is she even alive? Why did she, whoever she is, abandon me? What was wrong with me?

FRAN: Nothing was wrong with you. I'm sure it ripped her in half, letting you go. I know she'd be incredibly proud to see you today.

*(MEG thinking, unconvinced.)*

FRAN: . . . . I've decided to move back to Seattle, to come back home.

MEG: You have? You are? That's a big move.

FRAN: You have no idea.

MEG: Then there'll be someone here to help take care of Dad.

FRAN: I don't think that's part of the plan.

MEG: Did you check the Notebook? It's like I'm playing soccer but the nets are gone. It's getting dark, I'm by myself, I don't know which way to turn. I need to go find another field that makes more sense.

FRAN: Look Meg, you can get on that train. I won't stop you. But I need you to know that I don't want you to go.

MEG: What does it matter to you? You've never even seen me before.

FRAN: *(takes deep breath)*
No. I did see you go from me once. And you were gone for a really long time. I don't want to see you go again.

*(MEG slowly gets it.)*

MEG: So . . do you have that scar?

FRAN: Oh, I have lots of scars.

MEG: Wait just a minute. Do you know how weird and screwed up this is?

FRAN: I'm still trying to figure it out.

MEG: My mother is my aunt and my aunt is my -

FRAN: I know, it's a twister. At least we kept it in the family.

MEG: And now you're coming and I'm going.

FRAN: You don't have to go.

MEG: Who are you bullshitting? You didn't mind seeing me go before.

FRAN: I just told you -

MEG: Yeah, right! No cards, no phone calls, no birthday -

FRAN: No Meg. Not a day has gone by that -

MEG: That what?! Why didn't you ever visit, even if you were like my aunt?

FRAN: We signed an agreement that I wouldn't. We thought –

MEG: What were you so afraid of?

FRAN: They were afraid you'd turn out like me. And I was afraid they were right. . . . She loved you more  than . . .

MEG: The last couple of years, things haven't been so great, between us.

FRAN: And is that so weird? How many of your friends are tight with their mothers right now?

MEG:  Well I don't think it's right, I don't think it was fair.

FRAN:  Welcome to the big world kiddo.

MEG:  Shit.  And my father.  Who is my father?

FRAN:  Lew is your father.

MEG:  You and Dad!  Oh my god, I can only take so much -

FRAN:  No-no-no, not your father.  Like Iris.  Lew is the man who raised you.

MEG:  That was close.

FRAN:  Sorry.  Didn't mean to -

MEG:  So who was my -

FRAN:  Someone I met at a party.  Never saw him again.  Pathetic, huh?

MEG:  Was it a good party?

FRAN:  You were the best part. . . Can I give you some advice?

MEG:  About parties?

FRAN:  No.

MEG:  Mothers and daughters?

FRAN:  No. Bathrooms.

MEG:  Bathrooms?

FRAN:  Don't sit near them.

MEG:  What?

FRAN: On the train. And sit facing forward. And set a big Russian novel and a coat on the seat beside you to keep weirdos away. You'll have a better journey. Trust me. In case you decide to go.

*(MEG looks at money, pondering.)*

## ACT 2, SCENE 7

*(Late Friday evening, three days later. Hospital bed has been removed. "WELCOME HOME MOM" sign remains in place. Urn with Iris's ashes is present. Funeral reception has just wound down. DIDGE, FRAN, LEW and MEG on. LEW is studying Notebook. Warm, supportive atmosphere.)*

LEW: *(to MEG; nods toward urn)* Do you think it's too late to scatter the ashes?

MEG: *(picks up urn)* Half in the garden?

LEW: That's what it says. And the other half in that wildflower meadow on Mt. Rainier.

DIDGE: She always did want to recycle everything.

LEW: And she thought bone meal was the world's greatest fertilizer.

MEG: But she didn't just scatter it. She would work it into the soil. I should know; I helped her enough times.

LEW: So should we?

MEG: To do it the way she would do it, which is the only way we should do it -

LEW: No other way.

MEG: - we need more light. So let's do it in the morning.

LEW: Okay. And then this fall, before the snows come, we'll drive down to Rainier.

MEG: *(sets down urn)* Mom would like that.

DIDGE: *(to FRAN)* Sure you won't have some wine?

FRAN: Never touch the stuff. Coffee's great.

LEW: Hey, you're in Seattle.

DIDGE: This Merlot is excellent with these cheeses. I can't tell what most of them are though. Which ones come from a cow, which from a goat, which from a sheep - some cheeses come from sheep don't they, ewes anyway?

MEG: I'm not sure where everything comes from. It's a problem I'm having lately.

DIDGE: What about horses?

FRAN: Horses?

DIDGE: Ever had horse cheese?

FRAN: Never heard of it.

LEW: In Mongolia, somewhere over there I think, they make mare's cheese.

FRAN: Doesn't sound very good, does it?

DIDGE: No it doesn't. Who brought these platters?

MEG: No one.

FRAN: Where'd they come from?

MEG: I made them. Dad helped. *(points to a cheese)* That one's from a goat.

DIDGE: It'd have to be a mother goat, right? What do you call a mother goat?

FRAN: *(trying to remember)* Nnnn, ninny?

MEG: Nanny!

LEW: That's right, a nanny.

DIDGE: Ninny, nanny, whatever, you two outdid yourselves.

MEG: It's not like a cheese platter is the height of cuisine.

DIDGE: No, I'm not kidding. *(points to a cheese)* Know anything about this one?

MEG: That's a "double cream Gouda".

DIDGE: Well it really is quite gooda.

MEG: Thanks. Do you think Mom is - would be - upset?

FRAN: Whatever for?

DIDGE: The reception couldn't have been nicer.

MEG: Not the reception, the cheese platters.

FRAN: We told you, they're great, even if we're not sure where they all come from.

*(MEG picks up Notebook with marked pages.)*

MEG: I don't know. In here she has two menus, one for a funeral reception in the summer and one for the winter. Cheese platters are for the winter menu.

LEW: But Meg and I decided to make them anyway.

MEG: I guess we really walked on the wild side didn't we?

DIDGE: Somehow I think Iris is delighted with your rebellion.

FRAN: Yes, I think so too.

LEW: I'm not tired. I think I'll clean up.

FRAN: I'd help, but I need to polish up my resume so I can drop it off with the School District in the morning. Didge is going to go over it with me.

DIDGE: Two pairs of eyes and all that.

MEG: Remember you can use my computer.

FRAN: I know where it is.

*(FRAN and DIDGE exit.)*

LEW: Hell of a day, huh?

MEG: Hell of a week.

LEW: Hell of a life.

MEG: I'm not tired either, Dad. I can help you clean up.

LEW: Things have been a mess around here, haven't they? I could use your help.

LIGHTS FADE. END OF PLAY.

# Future Imperfect

a play by ،

## DUANE KELLY

## CHARACTERS

THEO, early 60s.  Father to Cristina, Luisa and Paulo; retired businessman.

CRISTINA, 36.  Professor of zoology who is world's foremost expert on penises of vertebrates.

LUISA, 32

PAULO, 29.  Performer.

BERTHE, 31.  Paulo's sexy German girlfriend.  Dancer, acrobat and contortionist.

MIRELLA, middle-aged Italian housekeeper, bossy, hands on hip, obsessive about her Catholicism, big heart under stern demeanor, not unattractive

POLICEMAN, 30s.  Italian, handsome.

## TIME

April 2008

## PLACE

A rental villa in the village of Bellano on the northeast side of Lake Como in northern Italy.  All scenes except one take place in a large room consisting of a dining area and a living area that adjoins a terrace.  Several doors lead off to other rooms.  One scene takes place in a small park next to Lake Como.

# *ACT 1*

## SCENE 1

*(Afternoon, Sunday, April 2008. Three Americans enter a villa they have rented for a week near Lake Como, Italy. They are jet-lagged and cranky, having travelled for 20 hours from Seattle to Frankfurt to Milan, and then by train to Bellano, a village on the northeast side of the lake. Struggling with their luggage, they descend a short flight of stairs into a large room divided into a dining area and a living room, which adjoins a terrace. Several doors lead off. THEO is unsteady on his feet. CRISTINA limps with one foot in a removable boot-cast. LUISA casts an eye about for a bathroom; her stomach is upset, a frequent condition for her.)*

THEO:  Well here we are.

CRISTINA:  Finally.

*(LUISA looks out window.)*

LUISA:  Wow, look at this view!  The lake's so blue.

CRISTINA:  *(joining LUISA at window)* So this is where Momma grew up.

THEO:  Well, the village anyway.  I don't think the Giovannis had the view property.

CRISTINA:  *(noticing that THEO is unsteady on his feet; gestures to a chair)* Come here; you're walking like a drunk.

THEO:  My balance has gone to hell.

CRISTINA:  Yeah, yeah, you told me on the phone.

LUISA:  Something's wrong in his vestibule.

THEO: Vestibular! My vestibular nerve is shot.

CRISTINA: Don't know it.

THEO: *(short)* Ataxia. And the staggering result *(mimes unsteadiness)* they call it ataxia. Maybe I should wear a t-shirt that says "I'm not drunk, I have ataxia."

CRISTINA: In Italian.

LUISA: Just don't "attax" us.

CRISTINA: Yeah, we're tired too.

THEO: Flying makes it worse. I'll be okay tomorrow.

LUISA: He'll only bump into doorways then.

THEO: Will you two lay off?

LUISA: *(grabbing her stomach)* Uh-oh, where's the bathroom? Villas have indoor plumbing, don't they? *(exits)*

LUISA (O.S.): Found it.

*(CRISTINA opens and closes doors, investigating the villa. She exits to kitchen.)*

CRISTINA (O.S.): Wow, there's an amazing kitchen!

THEO: What? I can't hear you.

*(CRISTINA returns.)*

THEO: My ears are still plugged from the plane.

CRISTINA: We're like the three lame, deaf and poopy mice invading Italy. Veni, vidi, winky, or however that goes.

THEO: What?

CRISTINA: *(shouting while mimicking Julia Child's voice)*
I was saying there's an amazing kitchen. Lulu can play Julia Child.

THEO: I think they call her "La Bambina Giulia" here.

CRISTINA: Momma would have loved that kitchen.

*(LUISA returns.)*

LUISA: The bathroom works.

THEO: Cristina has done reconnaissance and reports a well appointed kitchen waits for its chef.

LUISA: No kidding. Where?

CRISTINA: Thattaway. There's another bathroom there too.

LUISA: Can't have too many of those.

*(LUISA exits to kitchen.)*

LUISA (O.S.): This is so fantastic!

CRISTINA: *(shouting)* I told you.

*(CRISTINA tries to go out to terrace.)*

CRISTINA: These doors are locked.

THEO: Try one of these.

*(THEO tosses keys to CRISTINA. LUISA returns. CRISTINA opens doors and goes out to terrace.)*

LUISA: Did you lock all the doors?

THEO: We've been opening them.

LUISA: At home. When we left.

THEO: Of course -

LUISA: What about the back door. Did you lock that?

THEO: *(not completely sure)* Yes.

LUISA: Are you sure?

*(CRISTINA re-enters.)*

THEO: Yes.

LUISA: How sure?

THEO: Stop it. I locked all the doors.

LUISA: I don't remember you checking the back door. The taxi was honking and you were yelling and we had to get our luggage out. I never checked the back door.

THEO: Luisa -

LUISA: The Gilberts were robbed at Christmas.

THEO: And the Gilberts never lock their doors.

LUISA: My point exactly.

CRISTINA: I'll bet they do now.

LUISA: I think we should call the neighbors.

THEO: Oh god no, we are not calling any neighbors!

LUISA: Why not?

THEO: Luisa, please try to relax while we're here.

LUISA: Why?

THEO: Because we're in a gorgeous villa in a gorgeous part of Italy and if you don't I'm going to march right down to that lake, scatter Momma's ashes and drown myself.

*(LUISA glares at them.)*

LUISA: Where are the ashes?

THEO: In that plastic thing in the tote bag.

LUISA: Where's the tote bag?

THEO: With the other bags.

*(CRISTINA and LUISA poke around the luggage.)*

LUISA: I don't see it.

CRISTINA: Dad, do we have a problem here?

THEO: Yes, your sister, big-time. It's with all our other stuff. *(looks around luggage)* Now I don't see it.

CRISTINA: This is just great -

LUISA: You've -

CRISTINA: lost -

LUISA: Momma!

THEO: Hang on, I had her when we got off the plane and then at customs because it was weird explaining that that was my wife . . . oh crap.

LUISA: Oh crap what?

THEO: There was a problem, in the bathroom, at the airport. . .

CRISTINA: What kind of problem?

THEO: I was having a problem with my balance, at the thing, you know, the urinal, and I accidentally bump the guy standing next to me. I guess that means something because he bumps me back and I jump and accidentally pee on him - just a little - and he starts yelling in Hungarian or Swahili or Polish or something.

CRISTINA: Where are the ashes!?

THEO: I'm thinking! . . . The urinal is down here *(gestures)* and the Pollack is over here and the shelf is up here and, oh shit, I think Sonia's still in the bathroom at the Milan airport.

*(MIRELLA enters unseen and observes these peevish Americans. She is holding a glass of wine, not her first that afternoon.)*

LUISA: That is the most unbelievably -

CRISTINA: Stupid -

LUISA: Idiotic -

CRISTINA: Thoughtless -

LUISA: Barbaric -

THEO: Barbaric?

LUISA: Thing you have ever done!

MIRELLA: Buongiorno.

CRISTINA: Who are you?

MIRELLA: No, no, no, who are you?

THEO: We live here, I mean, we don't live here, but we're staying here, for one week. We're from America.

MIRELLA: You are the family of Church?

LUISA: Well, we're the Churches.

MIRELLA: You are not here until tomorrow.

THEO: No, as you can see, we are here today.

MIRELLA: You are here on Monday. Today is Sunday.

THEO: No, we left Seattle on Saturday and we got here today. Today is Sunday, right?

MIRELLA: I know today is Sunday but tomorrow is Monday and Monday is when you are here.

THEO: *(fumbles for, finds and holds up paperwork)* Here. From Mr. Gozzi, in Rome. That's who I've been dealing with. Who are you?

MIRELLA: Mirella.

*(Beat.)*

THEO: Yes?

MIRELLA: I take care of the villa.

THEO: That's nice but -

CRISTINA: We don't need any cleaning today.

MIRELLA: I live here.

THEO: I am sorry but no, we do, for the next week.

MIRELLA: I have appartamento downstairs.

CRISTINA: You do?

THEO: Wait a minute. *(mumbles as he skims the fine print in the rental agreement)*

LUISA: Are there any more of you?

MIRELLA: *(to LUISA)* No, no more. God answered my prayers; my husband Gino *(crosses herself)* die last winter.

LUISA: Oh, I am sorry.

MIRELLA: No sorry, I was happy to shovel dirt on his grave.

LUISA: Oh.

THEO: This says we have exclusive use of the villa. *(continues mumble-reading for another beat)* Here, "Fully furnished. Maid services provided."

MIRELLA: Si. And who do you think I am?

THEO: That's what I'm trying to figure out.

MIRELLA: I am the maid with the services. The maid who lives in appartamento downstairs and guards villa from crazy foreigners that stupid Signor Gozzi rents to. He drinks too much and does not need the money.

CRISTINA: Does your boss know you think he's stupid?

MIRELLA: He is a man.

LUISA: She's got a point.

THEO: *(defensive)* Hey!

*(MIRELLA gestures "You make my case perfectly.")*

LUISA: Uhh-ummm. *(mouths "Momma" to THEO)*

THEO: Right. *(to MIRELLA, grasping for her name)* Listen, M-mm . . .

MIRELLA: Mirella.

THEO: Yes, Mirella, listen, I need to get back to Milan immediately. We have a –

LUISA: Shhh!

MIRELLA: Why shhh? What is wrong?

*(Confused glances all around; CRISTINA points to her stomach and then to LUISA, indicating that's the problem. LUISA nods and grabs her stomach.)*

MIRELLA: *(to LUISA)*
Capito. I fix you. *(exits to kitchen)*

LUISA: No, that's - *(too late, Mirella's gone)* Shhh! Don't say anything about the ashes.

CRISTINA: Why not?

LUISA: Do you know what Italian jails are like?

CRISTINA: What?

LUISA: Do you even know if it's legal to scatter ashes here? Do we really want to spend the next ten years in an Italian jail?

CRISTINA: That is so ridic -

LUISA: Shhh!

*(MIRELLA returns with a glass containing cloudy liquid and a plate on which is one large olive.)*

MIRELLA: Here, good for - *(rubs stomach)*

LUISA: Oh, no thank you -

MIRELLA: Here –

LUISA: I don't think so.

MIRELLA:  Special drink, I make, for the stomach.

LUISA:  Thanks but no.

MIRELLA:  But yes.

LUISA:  No.

MIRELLA:  Yes!

LUISA:  Well, okay, if you insist.

MIRELLA:  No people are sick in my villa.

LUISA:  Right.

*(LUISA takes glass and olive. Starts to drink.)*

MIRELLA:  NO!

*(ALL alarmed.)*

MIRELLA:  First olive.

*(LUISA follows orders. The liquid tastes foul but, fearing Mirella, she drinks it.)*

THEO:  What exactly was in that drink?

*(MIRELLA glares at him.)*

CRISTINA:  *(to THEO)* Uh-umm.

THEO:  Oh.  And I really need a taxi.  Can you –

CRISTINA:  You're not going alone, not after losing -

LUISA:  Cristina!

MIRELLA:  Mario bring you here?

CRISTINA:  Mario?

MIRELLA:  If you come from station in red Opel, you come with Mario.

THEO:  It was red.

MIRELLA:  *(looks at her watch)* Now he watches football.

THEO:  Will you please call him?

MIRELLA:  At the taverna. *(mimes drinking)*

CRISTINA:  We need you to call.

LUISA:  Please.

MIRELLA:  Taxi to Milano molto costoso. *(rubs fingers to indicate money)*

THEO:  That's okay, this is a grave emergency.

*(CRISTINA and LUISA glare at THEO for his unintentional pun.)*

MIRELLA:  *(looks at her watch again)* Hmmm, Mario watches football one hour now.  He maybe cannot drive.

THEO:  Then he can sit in the back and give directions while I drive.

CRISTINA:  In your condition?

LUISA:  You can't stand up straight -

CRISTINA:  And you pee on strangers.

MIRELLA:  *(in Italian)* Comé?

THEO:  *(to LUISA and CRISTINA)* Will you lay off?!  We need to get back to Milan before she goes in the garbage or flies to China.

MIRELLA:  Who goes in China garbage?

THEO, CR. & LUISA:  No one!

THEO:  Listen, Mirella, please, I just need to get back to Milan.

MIRELLA:  I call Mario. *(crosses herself)* Buona fortuna. *(exits to kitchen)*


## ACT 1, SCENE 2

*(Early next morning, Monday.  An occasional cat's meow can be heard outside.  Dining table is set for breakfast. LUISA fusses with dishes on the table, waging an internal struggle.  Her compulsion for order wins: she furtively pulls out a small tape measure and adjusts the distances between the plates and glasses just so.  THEO enters unseen, holding cup of coffee, witnesses Luisa's weird behavior which he's seen before.  Embarrassed for her, he exits unseen; re-enters, first making noise to alert LUISA to his presence.  LUISA hides the tape measure and moves from the table.)*

THEO:  Good morning.  You make the coffee?

LUISA:  Hi there.  Yeah.

THEO:  Thanks.

LUISA:  How'd you sleep?

THEO:  By the time I fell in bed I was comatose.  You?

LUISA:  Not so great.  I had trouble getting back to sleep after you came home.

THEO:  What a way to begin our trip.  Mario thought he won the lottery.

LUISA:  Was Cristina any help?

THEO:  I think the guy in lost-and-found thought she was cute.

LUISA:  She must not have told him what she does for a living.

THEO:  No.  She did help keep me from falling over.

LUISA: Cristina's one of those people who knows they were put here for a reason.

THEO: Come on Lu. She's not exactly stable now either, at least her one foot. We all have the staggers one way or another. *(feigns losing his balance)* It's just that she's in L.A. so we don't get to see hers. How's your tummy?

LUISA: Fine.

THEO: You know, I'd like to see you try to pull yourself together.

LUISA: You're worried about me?! The man who loses dead people and pees on strangers. I'm fine. Everything's fine. What's not fine? Like you said, we're in a gorgeous villa in gorgeous Italy. *(flips from sarcastic to sad)* Without even Momma's ashes.

THEO: Aw, honey. The airport people said she'll probably turn up.

LUISA: Right.

THEO: They have our address here and my cell number. . . . Are you missing Tim?

LUISA: Not a chance. His new idiot girlfriend will find out soon enough that he'll make a pass at any fire hydrant.

THEO: You're going to meet someone who will sweep you off your feet and you'll have beautiful children and I'm going to spoil the hell out of them.

LUISA: Have you completely lost your mind?!

THEO: No, just Momma's ashes. That's more than enough right now.

LUISA: *(holding back tears)* Do you know why I married him?

THEO: Not a clue.

LUISA: Me neither. *(crying)* I'm so sorry I didn't listen to her.

THEO: She tried to warn you.

LUISA:  You didn't.

THEO:  Like you would have listened?

LUISA:  I would give anything now to have her in my face saying "I told you so." *(regains composure)* I think I hear Cristina getting up.

THEO:  I'm glad one of us can hear. *(taps his ear in unsuccessful effort to unblock it)*

LUISA:  Croissants and scrambled eggs all right?

THEO:  I'm fine with a croissant.  Does her royal Italian highness know you invaded the kitchen?

LUISA:  We have full use of everything. . . . Do you really think Paulo's going to show?

THEO:  No idea.  It's been so long since we've all been together.

LUISA:  We still won't all be together.  It would be weird seeing him.

THEO:  And then some.  I'm sure he has his staggers too.

*(Louder meows from outside.)*

LUISA:  It's been doing that all morning.  I wish he'd go away.

*(LUISA exits, can't stop herself from adjusting a plate on the way out.  THEO, worrying about her, watches her leave.)*


## ACT 1, SCENE 3

*(Later that morning.  CRISTINA and LUISA are clearing dishes from dining table. THEO is doing goofy-looking PT exercises for ataxia.)*

THEO:  Hey Lu.

LUISA:  Yeah.

THEO:  You know what would make this trip the best ever?

LUISA:  Yeah, carrying out Momma's wishes.

CRISTINA:  But first we'd need Momma.

THEO:  Yes, well, of course.  I mean besides that.

LUISA:  Fixing your vestibule.

THEO:  It has to do with the stomach, not the ears.  Come on, guess.

*(No response.)*

THEO:  Pumpkin gnocchi. . . Sonia was the world's finest cook and you were the finest student of the world's finest cook.  Of the thousand and one things Momma made, her best was pumpkin gnocchi.

CRISTINA:  Nuh-uh, tortellini with sun dried tomato pesto.  Ummm!

THEO:  Hey, be quiet, I'm working a deal here.

LUISA:  *(buying in)* It was the sage butter that put her gnocchi over the top.

THEO:  So what would it take to get you to make that?  With the sage butter. . . Come on, Lu, don't make a man who falls over beg.

LUISA:  I don't know if I can round up the ingredients.

THEO:  We're in Italy for chrissakes.

LUISA:  Well -

*(LUISA sees a mouse scurry.  CRISTINA also glimpses it before it disappears.)*

LUISA:  Yikes!

CRISTINA:  Ooh yuk!

THEO:  What?

LUISA:  You didn't see?

THEO:  See what?

LUISA:  I am not staying here.

CRISTINA:  There are mice in the "gorgeous villa".

THEO:    Really?  .  .  .  Well  this  is  a  really  old  house;  I'm  guessing
late-eighteen-hundreds.

CRISTINA:  What does that have to do with mice?

LUISA:  Once you have them they reproduce like rats, well they are rats, rats without steroids. Rats that have been breeding since the eighteen hundreds.

*(Cat meows outside.)*

CRISTINA:  See, he knows his dinner's in here.

*(MIRELLA enters. Disapproves of LUISA and CRISTINA clearing dishes; that is her
domain. Takes dishes from them. Notes their anxiety.)*

MIRELLA:  I do that. What is the problem?

*(Cat is heard again. LUISA, CRISTINA and THEO exchange looks: Should they tell
Mirella about the mouse?)*

MIRELLA:  Ignore the cat. It lives in the streets. Do not feed it or it will never
go away. And do not answer the phone.

*(ALL exchange "Whaaat?" look.)*

CRISTINA:  Sometimes cats can be useful.

MIRELLA: When? They dig in the garden and kill the birds.

LUISA: What if there were mice around? Wouldn't a cat be helpful then?

MIRELLA: Yes, if there were mice around.

THEO: I'm going to take a shower.

MIRELLA: You may have *(looks at watch)* five minutes.

CRISTINA: What?

THEO: Why?

MIRELLA: You want your girls to have hot showers too?

THEO: Oh, right.

CRISTINA: Eighteen-hundreds, remember?

THEO: *(remembering as he starts to exit)* Uhh, Mirella, we may have another guest arriving.

MIRELLA: More work, no more pay. That's life with Signor Gozzi. Who is other guest?

LUISA: Our brother.

CRISTINA: Maybe.

MIRELLA: Maybe he is your brother? At least he does not come early. Everyone must take short showers. *(to THEO)* Follow me. I show you how to use it.

THEO: I think I can figure it out.

MIRELLA: No, you cannot.

*(MIRELLA and THEO exit. Cat meows again, louder this time. CRISTINA goes to table, pours milk into a bowl, puts bowl outside front door, returns, closes door. Meowing stops.)*

CRISTINA: I don't care what she says, this "gorgeous villa" has mice.

LUISA: Agreed. If we stay, so does the cat.

*(Knocking at door. CRISTINA and LUISA exchange looks.)*

CRISTINA: Smart cat.

*(CRISTINA opens door. It is PAULO. CRISTINA and LUISA are not quite sure.)*

CRISTINA: Paulo?

PAULO: Come on, I haven't changed that much. Give me a hug!

*(PAULO goes to hug CRISTINA. Still uncertain, she accepts hug but quickly disengages.)*

PAULO: Luisa! Come here, it's your little brother.

*(PAULO hugs her too. Like Cristina, LUISA is tentative.)*

LUISA: We weren't sure you'd really show.

PAULO: I left Munich before dawn and the roads were wide open so I just drove straight through. I figured seven years is long enough.

CRISTINA: It's been eight years.

PAULO: Has it really?

LUISA: Yes it has.

CRISTINA: Really.

PAULO: Even more reason to come.

CRISTINA: We just appreciate that you could fit us in.

PAULO: So when did you get here?

CRISTINA: Eight years after you.

LUISA: Okay Cristina. *(to PAULO)* Yesterday.

CRISTINA: But the maid thought we were coming today. There were calendar issues. You can understand that - all those years having zoomed by like they did.

PAULO: Is Dad here?

CRISTINA: He's taking a shower.

LUISA: A short one.

CRISTINA: With the maid.

PAULO: Oh, great, will I get a turn?

*(CRISTINA and LUISA are not amused.)*

PAULO: Umm, how was your flight?

CRISTINA: It was a long haul - about twenty hours. Luisa got sick.

LUISA: Only when the man behind me almost dies.

PAULO: Really?

LUISA: Luckily there was a doctor onboard. Turns out this guy is having a panic attack. The doctor gives him pills that calm him down but he won't give me any so I order a double martini and pray we don't have to make a detour to Iceland or Greenland or one of those Lands you fly over on the way here. Then I get sick. *(looks at blouse ruefully)* I don't know that I'll get on a plane again.

PAULO: Well we didn't hit one traffic jam.

CRISTINA:  How nice for you.

LUISA:  Wait a minute - "we", you said "we".

PAULO:  Oh, did I?  Yes, well I was driving. . . . but, well, I came with my girl-friend, Berthe.  She drove down with me.

CRISTINA:  And where is Fraulein now?

PAULO:  At a cafe on the edge of town.  She's nervous about meeting my family, well not just her, and I - we - wanted to make sure it was all right if she's with me. I mean, it's been a lot of years and I really don't know what everyone has turned into, so to speak.

CRISTINA:  Well, we're still your sisters.

LUISA:  And you're still our brother, right?

PAULO:  You sure about that?

CRISTINA:  Sort of.

LUISA:  Go on, go get her, we want to meet her.

PAULO:  Okay, I -

(Paulo's cell phone rings.  He holds up his finger to LUISA and answers phone.  During phone conversation he is increasingly disappointed.)

PAULO:  Hallo Hans. Ja, ich bin in Bellano, am Comer See . . . Oh . . . Mist . . . Aber wir hatten die Zusage . . . Okay . . . Weiss das Berthe? . . . Ja, ich werde ihr es sagen . . . Ja . . . Bis bald. (ends phone call)

PAULO:  Shit.  Our company had a gig in Cologne and it just fell through.

LUISA:  I'm sorry.

CRISTINA:  You have a company?

PAULO:  Yes, well sort of.

CRISTINA:  Won't Dad be impressed?

PAULO:  It's not that kind of company.

LUISA:  What kind of company?

PAULO:  Look, it's complicated, and that call was really bad news. Let me go get Berthe and then we'll have lots of time to catch up. Okay?

CRISTINA and LUISA:  Okay.

PAULO:  See you in a few.

*(PAULO starts to exit, hesitates, comes back and gives CRISTINA and LUISA a quick kiss on the cheek.)*

PAULO:  It's good to see you.

LUISA:  Hurry back this time.

*(PAULO exits.  Beat.)*

LUISA:  Now what do we do?

CRISTINA:  Wait?

LUISA:  We gave him the room with the single bed.

CRISTINA:  Oh, right.

LUISA:  One of us needs to switch.

CRISTINA:  Lu, I really need a desk to finish my book.

LUISA:  Well, I need to be near the bathroom and -

CRISTINA:  You can run to the bathroom.  I can't run -

*(MIRELLA rushes in, shocked and angry, holding large illustrations she found in Cristina's room. Throws the pages on the floor. CRISTINA, furious, hop-hobbles and picks them up.)*

MIRELLA: What kind of people are you?!

CRISTINA: Don't you throw those!

MIRELLA: This is a Christian country. You cannot do that here.

LUISA: Do what?

MIRELLA: *(beside herself)* Arrghh! You must leave.

CRISTINA: What? What are you talking about?

MIRELLA: Or I call police!

LUISA: What is going on?!

MIRELLA: This! Pornografia!

*(MIRELLA holds up one page that illustrates primate penises.)*

CRISTINA: That is science!

MIRELLA: *(scoffs)* That is pornografia and it is against the law in Italia. I call the police and the priest!

CRISTINA: What have you done to these?!
*(holds out a page that Mirella has damaged with cleaning fluid)*

LUISA: You can't just kick us out.

MIRELLA: Atheists! Criminals!

*(MIRELLA telephones police.)*

MIRELLA:
*(to police on phone)*
Questo e Mirella al
Signor Gozzi villa.
Criminali sono qui. . .
Sex criminals. . .
America, like the Mafia.
*(to CRISTINA)*
I want you out of my villa!

CRISTINA:
I am a scientist! I am not
a criminal!
What I do is about as far
from "pornografia" as
you can get. Si, pornografia. From
LUISA
She is telling the truth. . .
I thought the mafia came
from here. Look, she
really is a scientist, a
world-famous expert in
her, umm, field.

*(to police)*
No, non lei. Ho bisogno
di voi qui, Pronto. Si, si.
Voila. Vi ringrazio.
*(hangs up)*

CRISTINA:
I am the authority on
primate penises!

MIRELLA: *(satisfied)* He is on his way.

CRISTINA: *(distraught)* I am writing a book and these are for that book and now you've ruined the book and probably my career along with it.

MIRELLA: I know about those books. That filth is on the Internet too. *(remembers statuette of Mary with Child on the wall; turns it around so Mary faces the wall; crosses herself)*

CRISTINA: You don't know anything about anything. You are a total, complete fucking idiot!

LUISA: I think she means you may have made a mistake.

CRISTINA: And we complain about Texas. . . Oh my god, what the hell am I going to do?! The manuscript is due by the end of this month, with the artwork.

LUISA: *(inspects damaged page)* Don't you have a copy somewhere?

CRISTINA: No I don't have a copy somewhere! *(to MIRELLA)* I can sue you.

MIRELLA: Ha! In Italia? Buona fortuna!

*(THEO, alarmed by the commotion, enters, one towel around his waist and another in his hands.)*

THEO: What the hell is -

*(POLICEMAN raps on the door and admits himself. He is on high alert.)*

POLICEMAN: Everyone stay where you are.

*(ALL freeze.)*

THEO: *(unsteady on his feet; catches himself)* Hello officer.

POLICEMAN: Is this drunken naked man the sex criminal?

THEO: I am not drunk; I have ataxia.

POLICEMAN: *(removing handcuffs from his belt)* Turn around.

THEO: What? You can't be serious.

POLICEMAN: *(more forcefully)* Turn around.

THEO: *(sputters)* But . . .

*(Comic business with towels. THEO and DAUGHTERS fear that waist towel will come loose. THEO tries to make waist towel more secure; doesn't know what to do with other towel. POLICEMAN finally gets handcuffs on THEO. POLICEMAN's good looks do not go unnoticed by CRISTINA and LUISA.)*

POLICEMAN: Buono.

THEO: I am not the criminal.

CRISTINA: What?!

THEO: I mean there is no criminal. Just one lunatic maid.

POLICEMAN:  I make the decisions.

LUISA:  *(distracted by the POLICEMAN's good looks)* How'd you get here so fast? Do you like live next door?

POLICEMAN:  Business is slow.  Not much crime in Bellano.  You want crime, go to Loica.

CRISTINA:  Where's that?

POLICEMAN:  Over the hill.  Half its people are crazy; the other half are smugglers.  *(confiding)* And they all cheat on their taxes.

CRISTINA:  I'm sorry.

THEO:  Excuse me.  Your father is naked in handcuffs.  *(to POLICEMAN)* What is this all about?

POLICEMAN:  I ask the questions.

THEO:  But -

POLICEMAN:  Please.  What is this all about?

*(MIRELLA and CRISTINA shove pages at him.)*

MIRELLA:  This is a disgrace to the Church and the State.

*(He examines the page from MIRELLA; it illustrates various views of a penis.  He next looks at the page from CRISTINA and is puzzled.)*

POLICEMAN:  This I think I recognize, though in my experience it's a little small.  But this?

CRISTINA:  Those are lateral views of the reproductive organs of the male brown-throated three-toed sloth.  Pretty dangerous stuff, huh?

LUISA:  She's a scientist.

MIRELLA: Don't let a slot fool you. That is pornografia.

CRISTINA: Just a minute, I can settle this.

*(CRISTINA exits.)*

THEO: Officer, my daughter is a leading authority on . .

POLICEMAN: Slots?

THEO: Well, yes, and all other vertebrates.

MIRELLA: What is vertebrate? They want to trick you.

POLICEMAN: *(to MIRELLA)* Per favore! I ask the questions. *(to THEO)* What is vertebrate?

THEO: *(hesitates)* It's like - not a worm.

MIRELLA: Worms! Hah!

*(CRISTINA returns, hands POLICEMAN her card.)*

POLICEMAN: Professor of Comparative Zoology, Cal-Teach.

CRISTINA: CalTech.

POLICEMAN: Pasadena. Where is Pasadena?

CRISTINA: In Los Angeles.

POLICEMAN: Near Disneyland?

CRISTINA: No, not really. Look I'm a scholar who specializes in male reproductive organs.

POLICEMAN: Is that correct?

CRISTINA: Yes that is correct. Those are illustrations for a book I am writing *(glares at MIRELLA)* that has to be finished in three weeks.

POLICEMAN: You teach this at university?

CRISTINA: Yes?

POLICEMAN: Why?

CRISTINA: Why not?

POLICEMAN: Italian women are experts without university.

LUISA: Oh, that's a different kind of expert.

POLICEMAN: Really?

THEO: Yes! She's famous, you know.

POLICEMAN: Well, she will certainly be famous in our little town.

CRISTINA: Is that really necessary?

POLICEMAN: Certamente; everybody knows everybody.

CRISTINA: Perfect.

POLICEMAN: *(to MIRELLA; holds up Cristina's card)* Have you seen this?

MIRELLA: No. Only thing I see is that. *(indicating illustrations)*

POLICEMAN: Amici, I think we have a misunderstanding. If I saw these I would be concerned too. *(with a smirk)* Particolarmente for the man with this.

CRISTINA: That's not a man, it's a slot, I mean sloth. Look, questions are fine. Damaging the artwork, accusing me of crimes, calling the police, that's not fine.

POLICEMAN: As I say, a misunderstanding. I thank you. It was a boring evening. *(to THEO)* Signor.

THEO:  Yes?

POLICEMAN:  These are your daughters?

THEO:  Yes.

POLICEMAN:  They are very beautiful.

MIRELLA:  There is also a brother coming.

LUISA:  Actually, he's already here, he's coming right back.

THEO:  He what?

MIRELLA:  *(sarcastic to POLICEMAN)* Maybe you will find him beautiful too.

POLICEMAN:  E possibile.

THEO:  Paulo's here?

CRISTINA:  Yes.

LUISA:  He was.

CRISTINA:  And then he left.

LUISA:  He has a surprise for us.

CRISTINA:  Yes, it's German.

LUISA:  He'll be right back.

CRISTINA:  In eight years.

LUISA:  With the surprise.

*(THEO is now completely confused.)*

POLICEMAN: *(to CRISTINA and LUISA as he starts to exit)* Perhaps we will meet again.

*(CRISTINA and LUISA are embarrassed and don't know what to say.)*

THEO: Signor! *(gestures to his wrists)*

POLICEMAN: Ah yes.

*(POLICEMAN releases THEO from handcuffs.)*

POLICEMAN: You may get dressed.

THEO: That was my plan.

*(POLICEMAN exits, scratching his head.)*

CRISTINA: *(to MIRELLA)* These, these drawings, you are never, ever to touch them again, do you understand? Capito? *(to THEO and LUISA)* That goes for all of you. If I don't get this manuscript in by the end of the month, my career is finito.

LUISA: Well, sure, but I think we're on your side.

CRISTINA: I just hope I qualify for unemployment. And Mirella, there will be one more person staying here.

MIRELLA: Si, your surprising brother.

CRISTINA: No, one more. There will be five of us.

THEO: *(still confused, counts his fingers)* Five?

MIRELLA: No. Five is too many, four is limit.

THEO: *(wanting to support Cristina)* No that's not right.

MIRELLA: The agreement says four.

THEO:  No it doesn't. *(takes paper from file, shows MIRELLA)* Here. It says up to six guests.

MIRELLA:  That is advertisement, not contract.

THEO:  *(pulls out contract)* The contract says the same thing. *(to CRISTINA)* Who is this fifth person?

MIRELLA:  Yes, who?

CRISTINA:  Our brother's friend.

THEO:  What friend?

LUISA:  She's the German surprise.

MIRELLA:  Wunderbar.

CRISTINA:  Her name is Berthe.

MIRELLA:  His wife?

CRISTINA:  We don't -

LUISA:  *(jumping in)* Yes, his wife.

THEO:  Paulo is married? And she died not even knowing -

MIRELLA:  Who died?

CRISTINA:  I think maybe they got married after that.

MIRELLA:  *(crosses herself)* Hail Mary full of grace. You must pay for extra food. And only water for four showers; short ones.

THEO:  Yes, yes, we understand.

*(Cat meows outside.)*

MIRELLA: And do not feed the cat. *(exits in a huff)*

THEO: I am very confused. I'm going to follow orders and get dressed. *(exits)*

LUISA: Paulo and his friend should be getting back soon.

CRISTINA: Berthe.

LUISA: *(getting weepy)* Do you think they're getting married?

CRISTINA: If it took eight years and Momma dying to reconnect with us, I doubt he's the rush-into-marriage type. What is wrong, Lu? I'm sorry, but you're a train wreck.

LUISA: I know; I'm a mess. You have no idea.

CRISTINA: Is that necklace Momma's?

LUISA: *(fingers it)* No. Yes. It was.

CRISTINA: With the diamonds?

LUISA: Maybe.

CRISTINA: I didn't know Dad was distributing her things.

LUISA: He's not.

CRISTINA: I see. So? *(no response)* Luisa?

LUISA: Momma gave it to me, right before she died. You weren't there or I'm sure she would have given you something too.

CRISTINA: We spoke on the phone lots and she never said anything.

LUISA: She joked that it was payment for my kidney. The real joke is that I give her a kidney and she dies. Do you want the other one?

CRISTINA: Necklace?

LUISA: No, kidney. Then we can both die too.

CRISTINA: Quit it. Your kidney added two years to her life. Now come on. Dad says you've been a disaster, you say you're a mess, and I'm looking at a train wreck. What is wrong?

LUISA: Everything's gotten all like way screwed up since Momma died. Like we used to live on Earth and now we're on Venus or Mars. Is Venus the one with the rings?

CRISTINA: No, that's Saturn. She died on what, a Tuesday, right? And the next morning, guess what? Wednesday showed up. That's how it is. And that's how it'll be when we exit. . . . Tears are exclusively human.

LUISA: That's all you can say - the next day was Wednesday and tears are human? What does that mean Cristina?!

CRISTINA: It's true, we're the only animal that weeps.

LUISA: Right now a biology lesson is not what I need goddammit!

CRISTINA: How am I supposed to know what you need - *(mimicking)* goddammit! . . . You've gone really weird on us.

*(Beat.)*

LUISA: That's how women get when they're pregnant.

CRISTINA: What? No. No no no!

LUISA: Four months.

CRISTINA: Luisa! Are you sure?

*(LUISA nods yes.)*

LUISA: You can't tell anyone. Promise?

CRISTINA: Isn't this the sort of thing people eventually figure out on their own? *(makes expanding stomach gesture)*

LUISA: Not if I like went into a convent. Aren't there lots of them around here?

CRISTINA: I don't think they do that anymore. What about Timber?

LUISA: He has no idea he sired a sapling.

CRISTINA: Have you thought about abortion?

LUISA: Momma would kill me!

CRISTINA: Momma's dead.

LUISA: Momma'd still kill me.

CRISTINA: You're probably right. Well I knew you were a train wreck but I never imagined a new caboose.

LUISA: I don't know what I'm gonna do. I'm living with my Dad, my stomach doesn't work, I'll be a blimp at your wedding, and in August I'll be holding a screaming baby with poopy diapers.

CRISTINA: You can poop and scream together.

LUISA: You are not being helpful. I don't have a husband and the baby isn't going to have a father.

CRISTINA: Marriage isn't everything.

LUISA: *(beat; pats her stomach)* It's a girl.

CRISTINA: Really? Are you sure?

LUISA: Good point. Maybe I should have shown you the ultrasound.

CRISTINA: You need to teach her that love is just a trick to keep the species going.

LUISA: What? You're marrying Professor Rob.

CRISTINA: Let's don't talk about him. You're not the only one with problems.

*(BOTH see mouse scurrying.)*

LUISA: Ughhh -

CRISTINA: Yuk.

LUISA: Get me out of here.

CRISTINA: Where's the cat when we need it?

LUISA: Uh-oh. *(grimaces and gestures toward her stomach, then toward bathroom)*

CRISTINA: No wonder your stomach's been touchy.

*(LUISA exits. CRISTINA is troubled. Knocks at the door.)*

PAULO (O.S.): Hello, anyone home?

CRISTINA: Come in.

*(PAULO cracks door to keep out cat. Cat starts to meow and continues until Cristina feeds it a few beats later.)*

PAULO: Can I let this in?

CRISTINA: No! She'll kill us.

*(With a struggle PAULO and BERTHE enter while keeping cat out.)*

PAULO: Determined little bugger, but I'm not sure she's a killer.

CRISTINA: Not her. Mirella, the tyrant disguised as a maid.

PAULO: Thanks for the heads-up. Cristina, I'd like you to meet Berthe, the love of my life.

*(CRISTINA and BERTHE shake hands. Meows continue outside.)*

BERTHE: Hello.

CRISTINA: We're so glad you could come.

PAULO: What about me?

CRISTINA: The cat was s'posed to take care of you. Speaking of which -

*(CRISTINA dashes into kitchen, returns with bowl of milk, cracks door and sets bowl outside. Meows stop.)*

PAULO: My sister the famous cat tamer.

CRISTINA: *(makes cutting motion across her throat)*
Mum's the word. The tyrant.

PAULO: Right.

CRISTINA: You didn't say she was beautiful. We haven't had time to get jealous.

PAULO: She is astonishing, that's what she is.

BERTHE: *(embarrassed)* Don't Paulo.

*(LUISA enters, weak and holding stomach.)*

PAULO: Luisa, this is Berthe. Berthe, Luisa.

*(LUISA takes just a step towards BERTHE; they trade little hand waves.)*

LUISA: So . . . you're from Germany.

BERTHE: Yes, Deutschland. And you are from America, ja? You come now because, because . . . *(realizes she's entered sensitive territory)*

CRISTINA: To scatter our Momma's ashes.

LUISA: *(emotional)* If we had her ashes. Dad lost them.

PAULO: You've lost them?!

LUISA: We didn't, Dad did.

CRISTINA: Luisa, try to pull yourself together. *(to PAULO)* Be careful.

LUISA: Stop making me sound like some fragile little thing that's falling apart.

*(CRISTINA gestures "Exactly.")*

LUISA: He's also lost his balance.

CRISTINA: She means that literally. If he starts to fall over, just get out of the way.

PAULO: Is that what happened? *(indicates her foot)*

CRISTINA: No, but I'm guarding the other one. The problem's in his ear.

LUISA: The inner one.

BERTHE: We will be careful.

PAULO: And hope you find Momma.

*(BERTHE notices Cristina's illustrations.)*

BERTHE: Impressive. Someone you know?

LUISA: Of course not.

CRISTINA: It's a generic example, and it almost got us arrested.

PAULO: Really?

LUISA: The police have already been here.

BERTHE: I was going to ask you to introduce me.
*(meaning the man whose specimen that is)*

PAULO: She's joking; she likes to joke. She's already seen the world's finest. But what are you doing with it?

BERTHE: Paulo, it is none of your business what your sisters do with those.

LUISA: She's writing a book, a textbook; that's one of the illustrations.

PAULO: Nooohhh. Seriously?

CRISTINA: Seriously.

LUISA: She's a professor of Zoology.

PAULO: My sister, a professor? Wow! What do you study?

CRISTINA: Zoology. *(pointing at the illustration)* Male morphology associated with the transmission of genetic information, to be precise.

BERTHE: *(aside to PAULO)* What does that mean?

PAULO: I'm not positive but I think she's an expert on cocks.

LUISA: Don't be crude.

BERTHE: Ja, listen to your sisters.

PAULO: Who are causing a crime scandal in Italy.

LUISA: Not me, just her.

BERTHE: Is that wunderbar thing God gave us, *(wiggles her little finger)* I mean us women, is it true that it's a miniature one of these? I ask you as a scientist, not as a woman. Although I am a woman.

PAULO: It's true.

BERTHE:  I have always wondered.

CRISTINA:  To oversimplify, they are developmentally related.  A baby born with external genitalia longer than two-point-five centimeters is considered male and the organ is a penis.

LUISA:  How big is that?

CRISTINA:  *(indicating with her fingers)* If it's less than that it's the wunderbar thing God gave you and the baby is female.

PAULO:  *(to BERTHE)* Have you ever measured it?

*(BERTHE is amused.)*

LUISA:  Don't be a creep.

PAULO:  What?  The only people who can live life not according to their own desires are those who have no desires.

CRISTINA:  What does that mean?

LUISA:  *(to BERTHE)* Do you understand him?

BERTHE:  No.  It's like we speak different languages.

PAULO:  Sei nicht albern.

*(THEO enters.)*

THEO:  Hello stranger.

PAULO:  Umm, hi Dad.  Berthe, this is my father, Theo.

*(THEO goes to shake Berthe's hand, loses balance, braces himself against something.  When he steadies himself, they shake hands.)*

THEO:  Don't worry, I'm not drunk.  Too early for that.  My ears have screwed up my balance.

PAULO:  They warned us.

THEO:  I do these exercises - oh never mind.  If I fall over, just stand me back up.

LUISA:  Unless he breaks his nose.

CRISTINA:  Then lay him back down.

LUISA:  On his back.

THEO:  *(getting a little peeved)* Hey, I may be falling over but I'm not the one falling apart.

LUISA:  *(erupting)* And I wonder who that could be?!  Just get off my back - everyone! *(storms off to kitchen, slamming the door)*

THEO:  *(shouting after her)* What is your problem -

CRISTINA:  Can we not do this?  She's really on the edge.

THEO:  No kidding.  If she'd listened to Momma and not married such a complete loser, she wouldn't be such a complete basketcase now.

CRISTINA:  Arghhh!

*(CRISTINA exits to look after Luisa.  An awkward beat as THEO and PAULO consider reconnecting.)*

THEO:  Paulo, not to put anyone on the spot, but what . . ? *(wags finger from PAULO to BERTHE)*

PAULO:  I can assure you she is not a loser.

THEO:  No one was suggesting . . . Are you married?

PAULO:  Oh no.  Berthe is my girlfriend.  Serious girlfriend.  We met in mime class last year -

THEO:  What do they mine in Germany:  copper, silver, what?

PAULO: Mime, a mime class.

*(PAULO does the glass box mime.)*

PAULO: We've been together ever since.

THEO: Got it. I can't hear either. I thought maybe you'd take up boxing. *(clumsily mimes boxing)*

PAULO: No.

THEO: Anyway, *(looks at BERTHE)* welcome, welcome, both of you.

BERTHE: Thank you. I have been wanting to meet all of you. Paulo is so unique. It has been hard to imagine his family.

THEO: Well, as you just saw, we have plenty of uniqueness to go around. . . I figured you must be brave, to be with him, but I hadn't expected beautiful. Maybe I should take a mime class. I could play a drunk.

*(THEO mimes a drunk; gets carried away and falls. PAULO and BERTHE help him up.)*

THEO: Thanks.

PAULO: So, Luisa has guy problems?

THEO: That's just one of the chapters you missed. Last year she married a lizard who was cheating on their honeymoon. Now she's living with me, temporarily I hope. In the meantime you should buy stock in Kleenex. She should be thrilled to see the last of Timber. I know I was.

PAULO: Timber? His name was Timber?

THEO: *(nods yes)* Cristina's doing better in that department. This summer she's marrying another professor. This one's in engineering. Maybe they'll go into business designing penile implants. So what are you doing these days - for a living?

PAULO: We have a company that performs -

BERTHE: Like between circus and theater.

PAULO: We don't use words much.

BERTHE: More acrobatics and mime and clowning.

*(BERTHE gives a quick demonstration, perhaps a small somersault.)*

THEO: Does this company make real money?

BERTHE: Not much.

PAULO: Not yet.

THEO: Part of being an adult is bringing home the bacon.

PAULO: I am twenty-nine.

THEO: You have responsibilities. *(meaning Berthe and a possible future family)* . . .
It took two months for my jaw to heal.

PAULO: My hand took longer. Turned out it was broken.

*(MIRELLA enters operating vacuum cleaner and ignoring their presence.)*

THEO: Hello! . . . HELLO!

MIRELLA: *(turns off vacuum cleaner)* Buongiorno.

THEO: We're talking.

MIRELLA: I am cleaning.

THEO: We see that. These are our other guests. This is Mirella; she runs the
villa.

PAULO: Ah, yes, my sister Cristina told me about you.

MIRELLA: *(crosses herself)* Your sister is going to hell.

PAULO: Ah; I'm sure I'll get there first.

MIRELLA: Take short showers. Your other sister knows the rules for the kitchen.

*(MIRELLA resumes vacuuming.)*

THEO: *(shouting over vacuum)* I'LL SHOW YOU WHERE YOUR ROOM IS!

*(PAULO and BERTHE get their bags and follow THEO out.  MIRELLA examines Cristina's drawings with a combination of disgust and curiosity, then turns them over. LUISA enters from kitchen, searching for her purse. LUISA tries to hide her distress. She becomes aware that MIRELLA is staring at her; she slips out to the terrace. MIRELLA realizes LUISA wants to be alone.  As she cleans MIRELLA unintentionally blocks access through French doors, trapping LUISA on the terrace.  When MIRELLA moves away from the doors LUISA starts to re-enter but then MIRELLA blocks access again.  This becomes a brief unintentional cat-and-mouse game, with MIRELLA oblivious.  Finally MIRELLA realizes that LUISA wants in, steps aside, LUISA re-enters.)*

LUISA: Thank you. . . I don't want to interrupt your cleaning.

MIRELLA: Signor Gozzi pays me to keep his villa clean.

LUISA: That's nice.

MIRELLA: Not nice. He pays me half that he should.

LUISA: I've lost my purse somewhere.

MIRELLA: Did you look in the study?

*(LUISA, agitated, looks in study, quickly returns, resumes searching living room. She is now obsessing about her purse.  Absentmindedly adjusts objects on a table.  MIRELLA indicates the drawings nearby.)*

MIRELLA: Are you in the same - business - as your sister?

LUISA: No.  She has made a career out of those. *(becomes weepy)* I've just ruined my life with them.

MIRELLA: *(confused)* Si, they ruin many lives.

LUISA: I guess they give her problems too. She almost got arrested, right? You still don't believe her?

MIRELLA: Why does a scientist waste time on those?
*(crosses herself; beat; sniffles as a polite excuse for LUISA's tears)*
Too many flowers here in springtime.

LUISA: What?

MIRELLA: You know, the flower dust. *(indicates her own sinuses)*

LUISA: Oh, pollen. I don't think that's the problem. *(holds her abdomen)* Where is my purse? I'm sure I had it down here.

*(LUISA frantically searches. MIRELLA is concerned about her. LUISA notices mountains in distance, goes to window.)*

LUISA: Those mountains, what's over there?

MIRELLA: Not your purse. That is Switzerland.

LUISA: Really?

MIRELLA: Maybe you go there some day. Not so good as Italy, but not bad.

LUISA: *(cynical)* Hah. I don't think there's much travel in my future.

*(The mountains increase LUISA's sadness. She grabs her stomach again. LUISA notices MIRELLA staring at her.)*

LUISA: Stomach problems, and future problems.

MIRELLA: You worry about the future of your stomach?

LUISA: Yes. And my life.

MIRELLA: Ah, capito. Maybe I can help.

LUISA:  Please, no more juice, not right now.

MIRELLA:  No, no, no, I have the touch.

*(MIRELLA touches forehead. LUISA twirls finger next to her own head to ask MIRELLA if she means nuttiness.)*

MIRELLA:  No; I can see the future.

LUISA:  Get out of here.

MIRELLA:  My aunt was famous for her power.  Before she die she pass gift to me.

LUISA:  You don't really believe that stuff.

MIRELLA:  Certamente.  When I am young she tell me I will marry a man who will hit me and I will have no children and I will live longer than him.

LUISA:  Then why did you do it?

MIRELLA:  *(ignoring the question)* She also tell me I will stay thin.  Three out of four is not bad, heh?

LUISA:  *(referring to the fortune-telling offer)* No, I don't think so.

MIRELLA:  The touch does not show everything; more it is a peek around the corner.

LUISA:  What about - ? *(points to the Virgin statuette, meaning Mirella's Catholicism)*

MIRELLA:  The Bible is full of people telling other people where they go.  Here.

*(MIRELLA arranges two chairs so they face each other.  BOTH sit.  MIRELLA pulls out garish fabric and ties it on her head in the fashion of a turban; crosses herself.)*

MIRELLA:  Close your eyes.

*(LUISA complies.  MIRELLA pulls out sachet, extracts a pinch of powder and sprinkles it over LUISA's and her own head.  LUISA coughs.)*

MIRELLA: Eyes closed.

*(LUISA keeps eyes tightly closed. MIRELLA takes LUISA's hands, closes her own eyes, hums strangely while focusing intently. A beat. MIRELLA becomes disturbed.)*

MIRELLA: I am so sorry; this is bad idea.

LUISA: No, now that we've gone this far, let's keep going.

MIRELLA: You are sure?

LUISA: Yes.

MIRELLA: *(refocusing)* You have recently suffered a great loss.

LUISA: Oh.

MIRELLA: Shhh. And you employ many tissues. . . After foolish mistakes you are now on a fresh journey. . . A new sky will be overhead with surprising new friends under it. *(concentrates more intently)* I am sorry. Clouds come; I can see no more.

LUISA: Please try. I have to know.

MIRELLA: *(concentrating)* I only see one thing more.

LUISA: What, what?

MIRELLA: It is very cold. *(shivers)*

LUISA: *(frightened)* Ohhhh, maybe I don't want to know.

MIRELLA: Your purse, it is in frigorifero -

LUISA: What?!

MIRELLA: Behind the eggs. That is all. I am sorry.

*(LUISA dashes into kitchen, quickly returns clutching cold purse.)*

LUISA:  How did you - ?  I don't know what any of that means.

MIRELLA:  Often there are clouds, even with the touch.
(touches her forehead)

LUISA:  Well, thank you, I guess.  At least we found my purse.

(MIRELLA shrugs.  LUISA exits.)


## ACT 1, SCENE 4

(Morning, next day, Tuesday.  Arguing by MIRELLA and CRISTINA escalates to yelling as scene progresses.)

CRISTINA:  Were you in my room?

MIRELLA:  When?

CRISTINA:  Last night?

MIRELLA:  Why?

CRISTINA:  I prefer you not go in there.

MIRELLA:  Why?

CRISTINA:  Until after we leave.

MIRELLA:  Why?

CRISTINA:  Because I still have a book to finish!

MIRELLA:  I know what kind of book.

CRISTINA:  No, actually, you don't.  Just stay out of my room.

MIRELLA:  It is my job to clean the villa, all the rooms.

CRISTINA: Let me be more clear: stay out of my fucking room. You can clean it when I'm gone.

MIRELLA: When you are gone I will boil the sheets and ask the priest to bless the house.

CRISTINA: I don't care if you get the Pope to bless your underwear.

MIRELLA: He is too busy to worry about a professional sex criminal.

CRISTINA: Professor, not professional! Just stay out of there while I'm here! Capiche?!

MIRELLA: Signor Gozzi pays me to make sure nothing is wrong. I go wherever I want! And right now I have work to do.

*(MIRELLA turns her back on CRISTINA and exits to kitchen.)*

CRISTINA: No you don't!

*(THEO, attracted by yelling, enters. CRISTINA hobbles after Mirella in hot pursuit and slams kitchen door behind her. THEO goes to kitchen door but lacks the courage to enter. He listens against door.)*

CRISTINA (O.S.): If you fuck with any of my papers one more time -

MIRELLA (O.S.): Get out so I can work.

CRISTINA (O.S.): there will be hell to pay!

MIRELLA (O.S.): You are one with hell to pay! Eternal hell. Get out!

CRISTINA (O.S.): You're crazy and insane, you know that?!

MIRELLA (O.S.): You write those books and call me crazy?!

CRISTINA (O.S.): You heard me!

*(CRISTINA storms back into living room, knocking THEO over.)*

CRISTINA: Arghhh! Someone's not going to leave this villa alive.

THEO: Probably me.

CRISTINA: What are you doing?! I'll bet she's related to Mussolini.

THEO: *(picking himself up)* Maybe, but she's not our biggest problem.

CRISTINA: You go in there and tell me that.

THEO: We've lost Momma and Luisa's headed straight for a breakdown. All she does is cry, lose her purse and move dishes around.

CRISTINA: She moves dishes around?

THEO: Oh wait 'til you see that, it's a doozy. She's gaining weight too. And she's so damned sensitive that if I called her on any of this she'd rip me a new one.

*(THEO's cell phone rings. He answers it.)*

THEO: Hello. Yes, this is he. . . I didn't have it turned on, sorry. . . Oh, thank God! . . . Where? Last night? Really? Grazie, grazie, grazie. *(ends call)* Momma's turned up; on a Lufthansa plane in Moscow. They have no idea how. Can you believe that? It's a miracle. And what's more, she's being delivered here right this morning.

CRISTINA: Maybe she was hungry for borscht.

THEO: Maybe. At least this solves one of our problems. Do you think if I flew her down to L.A. she could stay with you for a few months?

CRISTINA: Momma?

THEO: Luisa.

CRISTINA: No.

THEO: For a few weeks.

CRISTINA: No.

THEO: A few days?

CRISTINA: No!

THEO: Why not? She could set the table.

CRISTINA: I don't have a dining room.

THEO: I'll have you know I'm not in such terrific shape myself.

CRISTINA: I'm not either.

THEO: Maybe if you were a little less of a scientist and a little more of a sister, you could lift her out of the hole she's in. *(cups his mouth and hollers to the floor)* Hel-lllooo down there.

CRISTINA: But her sister is a scientist; sorry. Maybe her problems are bigger than we know.

THEO: Good; optimism is always good.

*(Theo's cell phone rings. He answers it.)*

THEO: Hello. Who is this? Hello Timber. *(rolls his eyes)* I can't hear you very well. . . Yes, that's because her cell phone doesn't work over here.

*(LUISA enters. THEO doesn't see her; CRISTINA does.)*

THEO: What's that? . . . She's not doing all that well. . . . Yes, she's here, of course. Well I mean not right here but here in Italy with us . .

CRISTINA: Uh-umm. *(points to LUISA)*

THEO: Oh sorry, she is here: here, here. You can talk to her, that is if she'll talk to you, but keep it short. . . . Because it costs about a thousand dollars a minute. . . . No, I'm joking, Timber; just a hundred a minute. Here she is.

*(THEO hands phone to LUISA.)*

LUISA: Forget it. You were my worst mistake and I'm going to be paying for it another twenty years. Oh really? Well, you might have a slight problem at the airport - because you don't have a passport you idiot! . . Yes, foreign travel is what they invented them for.

*(PAULO enters.)*

LUISA: Stop it. You can whack your wood there. . . No - go fuck yourself!

*(LUISA frantically pushes buttons on phone.)*

LUISA: How do you turn this stupid thing off?!

THEO: Here, you're gonna break it.

*(LUISA throws phone on the carpet toward THEO. THEO retrieves phone.)*

THEO: That's not what I meant.

LUISA: If he calls again tell him, tell him I went, went to Tibet!

PAULO: Tibet?

LUISA: And entered a convent.

CRISTINA: They don't have convents in Tibet.

LUISA: We're talking about a man named Timber who doesn't know you need a passport. Fine! Tell him I was kidnapped by a guru on an elephant who took me to a cave in the Himalayas and made me his sex slave.

*(ALL stare at LUISA.)*

LUISA: What?!

THEO: Gurus don't ride elephants.

CRISTINA: Flying carpets maybe.

PAULO: And they're not supposed to have sex, I don't think.

LUISA: What do you know about gurus? You went AWOL for eight years; I think I'm entitled to disappear for one or two.

PAULO: Europe is a lot more believable than a Himalayan cave.

CRISTINA: Not to mention comfortable.

THEO: *(to PAULO)* No one's gonna top your disappearing act.

LUISA: You're all giving Timber way too much credit. He has wood for brains. He's in the running for the world's stupidest man.

PAULO: Hey, I made it to the semifinals.

*(LUISA becomes emotional and remains so through rest of scene.)*

LUISA: And I'm the stupidest - [woman]

CRISTINA: Lu, this is our family. What you see in this room. I know we aren't much but it's what we've got. Certain things are going to become obvious -

LUISA: No!

CRISTINA: Okayyyy. You won't be able to keep it under your belt forever.

LUISA: Shut up!

CRISTINA: It's going to come out eventually.

LUISA: I said shut up! I hope you break your other foot.

THEO: *(reprimanding)* Luisa, you need a time-out!

LUISA: You can't talk to me like that!

THEO: Calm down now.

LUISA: No! Shit! . . . She's talking about someone else. . . . Momma's not here and I'm all alone and I don't know what's going to happen, because - *(blurts)* Okay, okay! I'm going to have a baby.

PAULO: No shit? You mean a real live - *(mimes rocking a baby)*

LUISA: Yes, a real live - *(imitates Paulo's baby mime)*

THEO: Are you sure?

LUISA: Yes I'm sure!

THEO: How do you know?

LUISA: Duh - I went to a fortune-teller.

THEO: Oh shit is right.

LUISA: Thanks.

THEO: When? *(imitates baby mime)*

LUISA: August.

THEO: My god. How could you let this happen, Lu?

CRISTINA: And don't forget who with.

PAULO: Umm, does Wood-For-Brains know about this?

LUISA: No! I wasn't sure I wanted to keep it, go through with it, I'm still not sure -

THEO: You can't do that to Momma; it would kill her.

LUISA: *(to CRISTINA)* This is family support?!

CRISTINA: She knows, she knows. Let's all try to be supportive here. She's pretty fragile right -

LUISA: Don't "fragile" me! It's so easy for you to stand there and talk about how fragile I am when you're so not fragile with diplomas up your PhD butt, about to marry some way cool professor. You two can go have perfect children who'll come out wearing those stupid-ass black square hats with those stupid-ass tassels and the tassels will hit your perfect kids in the nose and they'll sneeze their way up the great ladder of life.

CRISTINA: Does anyone have Xanax?

LUISA: For who?

*(CRISTINA gives LUISA a "Duh" look. BERTHE enters, discomfiting LUISA further.)*

LUISA: Just leave me alone, all of you!

*(CRISTINA sits. Her pant legs rise, revealing silly socks.)*

PAULO: Do those go with the stupid-ass hats?

CRISTINA: A Christmas gift.

BERTHE: I love them.

CRISTINA: Rob gave them to me - right before we broke up. *(to LUISA)* You're not the only one with problems.

THEO: You're not pregnant too?

BERTHE: Who's having a baby?

PAULO: Shhh, not now.

CRISTINA: No, thank god.

THEO: Thank god is right.

*(Knocking at door.)*

THEO:  I think I know who it is.

*(THEO walks unsteadily to door and opens it.  A deliveryman, who can't be seen, has the ashes.)*

THEO:  Yes, the airport called.  We are so grateful.  Here.

*(THEO hands a healthy tip to deliveryman.  Turns to OTHERS, removes ash container from box, opens lid to make sure ashes are there; smiling, kisses the container.)*

THEO:  *(to container)* Welcome home. *(to OTHERS)* Momma's back.  I better set her down. *(sets container on table)* She flew in from Moscow.  Really.  Let's just be glad she's back.

*(A beat of silent amazement at the ashes.)*

THEO:  Cristina, we're sorry.  You and Rob, do you mean totally broke up?

CRISTINA:  Yes, like totally, completely broke up.  Last winter I found a slight problem.

THEO:  How slight?

CRISTINA:  Polygamy is illegal, at least in California.

*(MIRELLA enters, prepared to do cleaning.)*

CRISTINA:  Can we not talk about this now?  She probably wants us out of here.

MIRELLA:  Si.

*(ALL exit to various places.  MIRELLA starts to clean.  Examines container with ashes. Thinking contents are dirt, she takes it outside front door and dumps on soil.  Returns with empty container.  Resumes cleaning.)*

(INTERMISSION)

# *ACT 2*

## SCENE 1

*(Later that same day, Tuesday. PAULO and BERTHE alone.)*

PAULO: I know, I feel sorry for them too. But is it any wonder they're both alone? Think about it. One is the world's leading expert on penises. The other is obsessed with measuring things. Can you imagine them on a double date? The guys couldn't run fast enough.

BERTHE: You never ran away from me.

PAULO: *(embracing BERTHE)* You're so right. My running was all in the other direction.

*(PAULO and BERTHE are quickly all over each other while murmuring love-speak.)*

BERTHE: You are such a strong runner.

PAULO: I always want to catch you. . . Here, and here, and here, and all over, to the finish line.

BERTHE: I like it when such a fine athlete catches me.

*(LUISA and CRISTINA enter from kitchen, each with a glass of wine, observe unseen. Their disdain covers envy.)*

PAULO: And hands you his baton.

BERTHE: Baton?

PAULO: Der Stock.

BERTHE: Oh, der Stock. He is panting so hard on that final lap.

PAULO: Oh and what a joyous finish line is ahead.

*(LUISA becomes emotional. PAULO and BERTHE become aware of them, regain their composure.)*

CRISTINA: It's awfully hot in here.

LUISA: Should we open the windows?

CRISTINA: Can you two turn it down a notch?

LUISA: *(to CRISTINA)* I mean, I'm supposed to avoid that sort of thing this next year.

CRISTINA: Yes that probably would be a good idea in your condition.

*(THEO enters. A mouse scurries.)*

LUISA: *(sees the mouse)* Ayyyghh!

THEO: I saw it that time.

*(Cat meows outside.)*

PAULO: Can't we just let it in so the two of them can duke it out?

CRISTINA: Have you met Mussolini?

PAULO: Oh; yes. She uses a vacuum like artillery.

*(Paulo's cell phone rings; he answers it. It is a theatrical producer in Milan.)*

PAULO: Hello. . . Yes, I'm him. . . Berthe Geiss, she's with me. We were booked for August but now we're free. . . We're actually quite close to Milan, visiting family through Sunday. . . Well let us know. Wait a minute, let me give you my number. . . Oh that's right, I guess you do. Okay. Hope we can meet. *(ends call; sings line from "42nd Street")* "We're in the money".

BERTHE: Okay, who was that?

PAULO: A producer in Milan who got one of our flyers. He wants to audition us.

BERTHE: Klasse! We need to rehearse.

PAULO: Ja, klasse, we need to rehearse the new act.

CRISTINA: What is your new act?

PAULO: We're still working on it, but basically, it takes place in the future.

BERTHE: There is this prince who refuses to be a hero.

PAULO: Even though his kingdom desperately needs him.

BERTHE: Because mutant chimpanzees have spread a worldwide plague and a meteor is about to crash into the Earth.

PAULO: And people start committing mass suicide like lemmings.

BERTHE: But all the men want sex first.

PAULO: The world as we know it is about to end.

BERTHE: Unless this prince accepts the challenge.

PAULO: It's a comedy.

THEO: Right, well let's hope for the best. We also need to plan the memorial service now that we have the ashes back. Momma wasn't expecting anything fancy. I saw a small park down at the lake that would be good and when we're all done speaking we can scatter the ashes the way she wanted.

LUISA: Speaking?

THEO: After we each say a few words.

LUISA: All of us?

THEO:  Yes, just a short eulogy, something simple from each of us, just for us. *(to BERTHE)* I mean you too Berthe, that is, if you want to.

LUISA:  I don't think that's a good idea.

PAULO:  *(thinking that LUISA is maligning BERTHE)*
What?  Why not?

LUISA:  No, me.  Public speaking turns me into a basket case.

THEO:  Well, certainly we want to avoid that.

LUISA:  And I need to think about the baby; avoid any emotional stress.

CRISTINA:  You're drinking wine for god's sake.

LUISA:  In extreme moderation.

CRISTINA:  That's not good for the baby.

LUISA:  Have you been to France lately?

CRISTINA:  No.  And you haven't either.

PAULO:  *(raises his hand)* We have.

LUISA:  Pregnant mademoiselles drink wine and you don't see a nation full of brain-damaged frogs.

BERTHE:  Uggh.  Frogs?

*(PAULO signals "Never mind" to BERTHE.)*

LUISA:  *(to BERTHE)* What do Germans do?

BERTHE:  Umm, I think this is a family matter.

CRISTINA:  He just said you're part of the family.

BERTHE:  But she is the scientist.

LUISA:  Weenies, not wine.

CRISTINA:  Could we please delete "weenie" from the nomenclature?

LUISA:  Just shut up, all of you.  I can have a glass of wine if I want.  Besides, it's Chianti.

CRISTINA:  *(a dig)* How does Momma's necklace look on Luisa?

LUISA:  *(to CRISTINA)* I told you -

CRISTINA:  Oh, right; on her deathbed.

*(LUISA rips off the necklace and throws it at CRISTINA.  It lands nearer to PAULO who picks it up, examines and retains.)*

LUISA:  Go to hell Cristina!

THEO:  Girls -

CRISTINA:  Don't "girls" us!

LUISA:  Yeah, just keep out of it.

THEO:  You're being impossible, I hope you know that.

LUISA:  Well excuuuse me.

PAULO:  Come on you guys. *(to LUISA)* You can say a few words.  Maybe have a little Chianti first.  Just write something simple -

LUISA:  So I can only do simple?  How long is her eulogy? *(meaning Cristina)*

PAULO:  At least you can say something you're proud of.

LUISA:  Like what?

PAULO: Oh, like you didn't abandon Momma and let her die not knowing if you were alive.

CRISTINA: And you were such a cute little boy.

PAULO: Like you gave Momma one of your kidneys. Somehow apologizing to ashes doesn't quite cut it.

*(THEO looks around for ashes.)*

THEO: Where is Momma?

*(ALL look around.)*

CRISTINA: What is it with the ashes?

THEO: They were just here.

LUISA: Did you take them to the bathroom again?

THEO: No I did not take them to the bathroom again! Mirella! Mirella, where are you?!

*(MIRELLA enters.)*

THEO: There was a plastic thing with this gray stuff inside. Now it's gone. Have you seen it?

MIRELLA: About this big? *(gestures)*

CRISTINA: Yes.

MIRELLA: Why?

CRISTINA: Because it's kind of important to us.

MIRELLA: Why?

THEO: Because it's their -

LUISA:  Because it's our favorite plastic thing.

MIRELLA:  It is in the kitchen.

THEO:  Where?

MIRELLA:  Under sink.

*(THEO moves toward kitchen.)*

MIRELLA:  The dirt that was in it, I put in the garden.

LUISA:  Dirt?!

CRISTINA:  In the garden?!

MIRELLA:  Yes, in the garden. *(points to front door)* In Italia that is where we keep the dirt.

*(ALL except MIRELLA hurry outside. CRISTINA immediately returns, grabs a newspaper, runs back out. A few beats later ALL return with flattened newspaper pages on which is a sad pile of ashes and dirt. When newspaper is set on table some ashes/dirt falls on floor and the FAMILY scrambles to retrieve.)*

MIRELLA:  I will get the vacuum.

                                    ALL
No!!!

*(FAMILY sits around table, thoroughly depressed over this sad pile.)*

CRISTINA:  *(to MIRELLA)* How could you be so stupid?

THEO:  This is their mother!

MIRELLA:  Mother?

PAULO:  Our Momma's ashes.

THEO: *(holding back tears)* And my wife.

MIRELLA: How could I know?

THEO: We heard horrible things about Italian jails.

*(ALL look at LUISA accusingly.)*

LUISA: Back off.

MIRELLA: Before you come I think Russians are the craziest.

PAULO: Our Momma was Italian. Like you.

CRISTINA: No, not like her.

PAULO: *(to CRISTINA)* Be careful, certainty in the face of complexity can be dangerous.

*(ALL look at Paulo like he's nuts.)*

THEO: Their mother grew up here.

MIRELLA: In Bellano? What is her name?

THEO: Sonia Giovanni.

MIRELLA: Oh, her mother was Allegra Giovanni?

THEO: Yes.

MIRELLA: Si, I knew her family. Your Sonia was a few years before me in school. Her mother Allegra could be difficult. No one was surprised when Sonia moved away. But what a surprise this is.

THEO: I'm sorry we didn't just tell you. We were trying to keep it private.

LUISA: She died last year.

MIRELLA: Oh.

PAULO: And wanted her ashes scattered in Lake Como.

MIRELLA: Ahhh.

THEO: Do you have a vase or something we could put Sonia in?

*(MIRELLA exits to kitchen.)*

CRISTINA: What can you expect from someone who thinks anatomy is pornografia?

PAULO: She didn't know it was Momma. I might have done the same thing if I was cleaning.

BERTHE: You have cleaned before?

PAULO: Everyone's just a little frazzled right now.

*(MIRELLA returns holding an odd-looking vase. THEO takes vase.)*

THEO: Let's try to do this with respect.

*(ALL begin to put ashes in vase.)*


## ACT 2, SCENE 2

*(Next evening, Wednesday. PAULO, BERTHE and THEO are doing exercises: Paulo and Berthe for performance, Theo as physical therapy for balance. LUISA is depressed. CRISTINA is on the villa's phone.)*

CRISTINA: I don't think I can help you. . . Yes, I am a doctor but not that kind of doctor . . . . No! You're wasting your time, I can't help you. . . . Hello? Hello? *(she has lost the phone connection; to THEO, BERTHE and PAULO)* Arghhh. It's somebody with the police. He says they have an emergency and need my help.

THEO: How big an emergency?

*(MIRELLA enters, returning from errands, carrying grocery bags.)*

CRISTINA: Apparently much too big. He's on his way here. *(to MIRELLA)* How many people in this town know what I do?

MIRELLA: Bellano is a small village.

CRISTINA: All of northern Italy appears to now believe that a penis-expert-slash-celebrity resides here.

MIRELLA: If that is what people think, it is your fault. Word travels molto veloce. Some are saying you are in those movies. You bring shame to the Giovanni family.

*(MIRELLA notices that the Mary statuette is turned the right way round. She turns it so it faces the wall again. Crosses herself.)*

CRISTINA: There is nothing shameful about them. They are serious -

PAULO: Cristina, you have to admit that if someone didn't know what your profession was, they could get the wrong idea.

CRISTINA: Oh when did you become a defense attorney? Butt out! This is between me and Mussolini.

*(POLICEMAN knocks and lets himself in.)*

POLICEMAN: *(to CRISTINA)* Good, you are here.

PAULO: Hello officer.

MIRELLA: Buona sera.

POLICEMAN: *(to THEO)* Nice to see you dressed.

CRISTINA: I didn't know it was you on the phone.

POLICEMAN: Bellano police department is not so big.

CRISTINA: I see. Look -

POLICEMAN: Will you please step outside, out to my car? I would bring the victim in -

LUISA: Victim?

POLICEMAN: But he bumped the door when I put him in the car and he started screaming and now I am afraid to move. Do you recognize these?

*(POLICEMAN hands CRISTINA pill bottle. She holds up a blue pill.)*

CRISTINA: Sildenafil; it increases blood flow.

POLICEMAN: Viagra.

CRISTINA: Yes, that's what Pfizer calls it.

POLICEMAN: Do you know the side effects?

CRISTINA: I'm not a medical doctor.

POLICEMAN: You are a doctor, right?

MIRELLA: No she is not.

PAULO: Yes she is.

POLICEMAN: A doctor who knows something about things *(points toward his groin)* down there. I have a man in my car screaming with a grosso problem. His thing has been *(struggles for right word, can't find it, so raises his forearm to indicate)* for six hours and he is in great pain. I have no experience in these matters. *(with a slight smirk)* I have never needed such pills.

MIRELLA: Let me see.

*(CRISTINA returns pill to bottle and hesitantly hands it to MIRELLA, who examines it with great curiosity.)*

THEO:  Umm, can I look at those? *(takes bottle from MIRELLA)*

CRISTINA:  *(snatches bottle from THEO)* No you cannot look at those.

POLICEMAN:  *(perturbed)* Let me have those. *(takes bottle from CRISTINA)*

CRISTINA:  What I am trying to tell you is that I'm not qualified to deal with this. You need to take him to a urologist.

POLICEMAN:  What is urologist?

THEO:  Harrumph. *(points to his groin and winks to POLICEMAN)*

CRISTINA:  A doctor who specializes in that sort of problem.

POLICEMAN:  We don't have a *(stumbles)* urologist in Bellano.

CRISTINA:  Then any medical doctor.

POLICEMAN:  I am afraid the only doctor we have in Bellano is *(reads from Cristina's business card)* una Professor of Comparative Zoology from Cal-Teach. You are the closest thing we have, especially for such problema delicato.

CRISTINA:  I'm sorry but I can't help you. Your car, does it have a siren and those colored lights?

POLICEMAN:  Si.

CRISTINA:  Well turn them all on and drive really fast to the nearest hospital.

POLICEMAN:  Will the beautiful doctor not come and look at him, per favore?

BERTHE:  I will.

PAULO:  Joking, just joking. She likes to joke. She does comedy.

CRISTINA:  You should hurry.

POLICEMAN:  Can it - ? *(mimes explosion)*

CRISTINA:  No, it won't - . *(imitates explosion mime)*

PAULO:  But just to be safe I'd keep him in the back seat, on the passenger side.

POLICEMAN:  What?

PAULO:  Just joking.

CRISTINA:  Hurry.

*(CRISTINA sees POLICEMAN out.  When she opens door the cat tries to come in.)*

MIRELLA:  Do not let it in.

CRISTINA:  We know!

*(CRISTINA, struggling due to her boot-cast, manages to keep cat out.  CRISTINA slams door.  Cat howls.)*

MIRELLA:  The cat has been worse lately.  Does anybody feed it?

OTHERS:  *(in unison)* No!

LUISA:  *(to MIRELLA)* Do you think there could maybe be a mouse problem?

MIRELLA:  Where?

LUISA:  Here in the villa.  Just one or two little mice?

MIRELLA:  There are no mice.

CRISTINA:  We think we saw one.

MIRELLA:  You did not.

CRISTINA:  Yes we did.

BERTHE:  I saw it too.

MIRELLA:  What do Germans know?

THEO:  We just thought the cat might be useful, in case there were mice, a mouse, a little mouse.

BERTHE:  *(with hand, mimes mouse scurrying)*
Ja, eine winzige Maus.

PAULO:  On the other hand, it could be a tomcat who took one of those blue pills.

CRISTINA:  I'm going to work on my book.

LUISA:  I'm going to my room.

BERTHE:  I need to rehearse.

THEO:  *(to MIRELLA)* Here, I'll help with those bags.

*(MIRELLA is pleasantly surprised at THEO'S gesture.  ALL exit except PAULO who is surprised to find he is alone.  Takes the necklace from his pocket.  Takes out cell phone and dials while holding necklace.)*

PAULO:  Hallo.  Na, rate mal, wer dran ist. . . Ya. . . I miss you too.  I don't like being away from you either.  You'll get a really big hug when I get back.  I'm not that far away. . . .  Hab dich lieb.  Seh dich bald.

*(PAULO puts phone in a front pants pocket.  Becomes reflective.  He picks up vase with ashes.  The cat outside makes an ungodly shriek, startling PAULO and causing him to drop necklace into the vase.  PAULO scans room to make sure no one is looking then reaches in to retrieve necklace.  Hand gets stuck.  Struggles to free hand but can't.  He perceives someone entering and hides vase behind his back.  BERTHE enters.)*

BERTHE:  What is wrong?

PAULO:  Nothing.

*(Paulo's cell phone rings in his front pants pocket that is opposite his free hand. His free hand can't reach the phone.)*

PAULO: Will you please answer the damn thing?

BERTHE: What is wrong with you?

PAULO: Just answer the phone; it could be important!

*(BERTHE tries to retrieve the ringing phone.)*

PAULO: Dammit, get the phone!

BERTHE: Schrei mich nicht so an!

PAULO: Well you're yelling at me!

BERTHE: Because you are yelling! Sei still!

*(As Berthe struggles, THEO, CRISTINA and LUISA enter, attracted by the noise. MIRELLA comes right behind them with a glass of wine. They are astonished to see PAULO squirming while BERTHE has her hand down his pants. Behind his back PAULO continues to hide the vase with his hand stuck in it.)*

CRISTINA: *(to LUISA)* I don't think they turned the heat down.

*(BERTHE finally retrieves phone and answers it. While she talks on phone OTHERS walk around PAULO and discover his predicament.)*

BERTHE: Yes. . . Yes he's here but I don't think, ummm, he cannot talk right now. I can take a message. This is Berthe Geiss, his partner. Ya, his artistic partner.

*(PAULO gives her a look.)*

BERTHE: Friday, nine-thirty, Milan, your office . . . No problem. Paulo has your address I think.

*(BERTHE glances at PAULO who nods assent.)*

BERTHE: Yes he does. . . Ja we can audition scenes from our new act. . . Bitte. . . Goodbye. *(to PAULO)* That was the producer. He wants us to audition. Yayyyyy!

CRISTINA: If we don't get his hand out of there there won't be any audition.

THEO: Don't try to punch anyone.

LUISA: *(with exasperation)* Oh, Paulo. Just a minute.

MIRELLA: The butter.

*(LUISA exits to kitchen and quickly returns with butter. Comic business as everyone works on PAULO's hand. Finally his hand is free.)*

CRISTINA: Great, now Momma has butter to go with the dirt.

THEO: She did like to garden and cook.

*(THEO grabs the vase and emphatically places it on a shelf.)*

THEO: Now no one, and I mean no one, touches that until the memorial service. All right?!

*(PAULO holds up the necklace, now covered with ash.)*

PAULO: What should I do with this?

CRISTINA: It's not mine. Maybe strangle yourself.

MIRELLA: Not in the villa.

BERTHE: Please wait until after the audition. We should do our exercises.

THEO: Me too.

CRISTINA: I need to finish my book.

*(CRISTINA exits. LUISA slumps into a chair, holding back tears.)*

PAULO: *(to BERTHE)* I'll be right there. I need to wash my hands.

*(PAULO exits. THEO and BERTHE resume their exercises. THEO's are stumbling, BERTHE's graceful. BERTHE's work gradually involves more contortions, some with sexual overtones. THEO soon stops to admire BERTHE's, which are so amazing that they make LUISA queasy.)*

LUISA: How can someone do that? I can't even stand to look.

*(LUISA grasps her stomach and hastens for the bathroom.)*

MIRELLA: Hurry.

*(LUISA points to her stomach as she passes PAULO who re-enters. PAULO proudly notices how THEO and MIRELLA are in awe of BERTHE. PAULO begins moderate exercises.)*

THEO: So this is the comedy where everyone kills themselves?

PAULO: If we didn't keep in shape, we'd never finish a performance. . .

THEO: Doesn't sound like any of your characters do.

PAULO: She's amazing, isn't she?

THEO: Amazing yes, and you're lucky.

PAULO: *(in a confiding tone)* I don't think she was luck. Some would call it luck, but I don't.

THEO: What do you call it?

PAULO: There's this place halfway between luck and fate, but I'm not sure what to call it. Maybe miracle, maybe miracle's the word.

THEO: What's a miracle is how your brain works.

MIRELLA: *(slightly tipsy; to THEO)* Your girls, they are very different.

THEO: Well, they're not twins.

*(LUISA enters unseen and stands aside.)*

MIRELLA: Luisa, she needs to stand on her own foot.

THEO: Feet. And lately none of us are standing so well.

MIRELLA: She needs to find a back. *(indicates her own spine)*

THEO: Backbone. There's a lot she's dealing with right now.

MIRELLA: Her sister, she trades in pornografia but she has a back.

LUISA: *(emotional; surprising ALL by her presence)* She does not trade in pornografia you ignorant cow and I do have a back - I mean backbone.

*(MIRELLA gestures "See what I mean?" and exits.)*

THEO: Maybe you misunderstood her.

LUISA: Come on! I don't have a back? What the hell does that mean?! I suppose that's what you all think.

THEO: She's just concerned about you.

PAULO: We all are.

LUISA: Sure you are.

*(LUISA crumples and sits. PAULO, when LUISA is not looking, signals to BERTHE that they should leave Luisa and Theo alone. BERTHE and PAULO exit. THEO, wanting to console LUISA but at a loss as to how, makes halting movements toward her. To dispel his awkwardness he resumes his exercises. LUISA slowly regains her composure but remains hurt.)*

LUISA: *(sniffling)* Do you think that guy with the, the blue pills is okay?

THEO: *(shudders)* Ughh, I don't even want to think about it. That's the last time I ever even - not that I ever -

LUISA:  I really don't -

THEO:  Of course.  Let's not.

LUISA:  Right.  Weird. . . Do you have to do those *(meaning his exercises)* for the rest of your life?

THEO:  I think so; I'd like to be standing up straight when my prostate goes, or my mind for that matter.  I'm hoping the kidneys hang in there.  You don't have a spare left.

*(LUISA doesn't respond.)*

THEO:  I think Mirella likes you.  And she maybe does have a point.

*(LUISA doesn't respond.)*

THEO:  It maybe would be good if you took more charge of your life.

LUISA:  So now it's time to play father?

THEO:  That's not fair.

LUISA:  *(looks toward ashes)* She would have remembered.

THEO:  What?  Remembered what?

LUISA:  What today is.

THEO:  It's Wednesday.

LUISA:  No, it's my birthday.

THEO:  Oh Lu.  I'm sorry.  I've been so upset over the ashes.  Dammit.  Life was so much simpler when she was here.  All I had to do was remember her birthday and she remembered everyone else's.

LUISA:  You remembered Cristina's last July.

THEO:  Only because Momma reminded me.  Hey, we can have a birthday party here, in Italy.

LUISA:  Right.

THEO:  No, we can, we really can.  We can celebrate it tomorrow.  That'd be only one day off.

LUISA:  We're taking the ferry to Bellagio.

THEO:  When we get back.

LUISA:  Nobody remembered.

THEO:  You don't know that.

LUISA:  Sure.  Three weeks ago Paulo didn't even remember he had an American family and all Cristina remembers is her deadline.

THEO:  That's not fair.

*(CRISTINA enters.)*

CRISTINA:  *(to THEO)* Can I borrow your cell -

LUISA:  Ask her.

CRISTINA:  Ask me what?

THEO:  Ummm, do you know if anything special's going on today?

LUISA:  Or not going on today.

CRISTINA:  I know that if I don't get this last chapter finished, I'm screwed.

LUISA:  *(to THEO)* What did I tell you?

THEO:  It's her birthday.

CRISTINA: Ohhhh. That's right, it is, isn't it? Happy Birthday Sis!

LUISA: Thanks.

*(PAULO enters.)*

PAULO: There you are.

LUISA: We're playing a game.

CRISTINA: *(to PAULO)* Be careful.

LUISA: When's your birthday?

PAULO: September thirteen.

LUISA: Well that's a start. When's mine?

PAULO: Uh, it's in the Spring, I'm pretty sure. April!

LUISA: April what?

PAULO: Got me.

LUISA: It's today. *(to THEO and CRISTINA)* At least he knew the month.

CRISTINA: No he didn't. He had a one-in-twelve chance and got lucky.

LUISA: That was better than you.

PAULO: Yeah, better than you.

CRISTINA: Psychologists have found that we demonstrate a high degree of selectivity in our recollection of facts.

LUISA: Okay professor, show off your big PhD words.

PAULO: It's not her fault she talks like a scientist.

LUISA: Why don't you go look for your *(uses German accent)* German sex on a stick?!

PAULO: How am I supposed to respond to that?!

LUISA: I don't give a damn.

THEO: Luisa, go to your room!

LUISA: You can't talk to me like I'm five years old!

THEO: I can when you act five!

LUISA: Ha! Wrong. I'm thirty-three, just in case you care, which obviously no one does.

PAULO: You're that old?

*(LUISA takes a plate and throws it on the floor, breaking it.)*

LUISA: The next one's gonna be on your head!

PAULO: Me?

CRISTINA: You didn't even know Momma was dying.

LUISA: I hope you have a child and he vanishes.

*(PAULO is stung by LUISA's curse.)*

CRISTINA: Then you'll know how Momma felt.

THEO: Momma died from her kidneys but you broke her heart.

PAULO: Stop ganging up on me.

LUISA: What are you going to do - hit us?

THEO: No one's ganging up on you.

LUISA:  Yes we are.  He was a little shit.

PAULO:  *(to THEO)* What do you call that?

CRISTINA:  *(to LUISA)* Who's going to be interested in you when you act like this!?

LUISA:  I don't see the boys lined up for you.

CRISTINA:  I think it's time for you to shut up!

LUISA:  No, you shut up!

*(CRISTINA moves toward LUISA intending assault.  She trips over her boot-cast and falls.  THEO goes to help CRISTINA, loses his balance and falls over her.)*

PAULO:  Everybody shut up!

CRISTINA and LUISA:  *(to PAULO)* Stay out of it!

LUISA:  I don't want to be around any of you!

*(LUISA grasps her stomach and starts to leave but her clothing catches on something, tearing off part of her clothing.)*

LUISA:  Arghhh!

*(ALL catch their breath and survey the war zone.  PAULO picks up the broken plate.  His dismay flips to laughter as he realizes how ridiculous they've been.  The laughter becomes infectious.)*

THEO:  I'm so glad we can have this time together.

LUISA:  It's really really special.

THEO:  *(to PAULO)* We were going to have a birthday party tomorrow night.  Do you and Berthe want to come?

PAULO:  Will we have enough plates for the cake?

CRISTINA: *(grimaces and reaches for her lower back)* Oh my back; I've twisted it.

*(PAULO goes to CRISTINA to offer support.)*

LUISA: Quick, hide that *(the broken plate pieces)* before Mussolini sees it and gets pissed.

THEO: If she didn't hear that lovefest she must already be pissed.

CRISTINA: I prefer drunk to despotic.

*(Laughter subsides but goodwill remains.)*

PAULO: I know, Berthe and I have been rehearsing for our audition. How about we perform our sketch for the party?

THEO: That okay with you, Lu?

LUISA: Can you skip the part where everybody commits suicide?

PAULO: We're leaving that out of the audition.

THEO: Probably a good idea.

*(MIRELLA enters in a pleasant mood, a little drunk. PAULO quickly hides plate behind his back. MIRELLA sees an affectionate family.)*


## ACT 2, SCENE 3

*(Thursday evening. The family has just returned from a restaurant. All except Luisa enjoyed plenty of wine at dinner and are drinking more wine at the villa. MIRELLA, though she didn't dine with them, is also well fortified. LUISA still harbors a grudge about her overlooked birthday.)*

THEO: Luisa, can you help out an old man? I forget what we're celebrating here.

*(LUISA doesn't cooperate with the effort to humor her.)*

PAULO:  Come on Lu.  On your birthday it's good to remember the difference between beer and wine.

*(ALL give PAULO a "What the hell are you talking about?" look.)*

PAULO:  No I'm serious.  You can make beer year-round but wine only once a year.

CRISTINA:  *(to BERTHE)* Do you really understand him?

BERTHE:  No, but he has eyes like a gypsy.

THEO:  Okay everybody, how young is Miss Luisa today?

LUISA:  Yesterday.

| THEO, CRISTINA & BERTHE: | PAULO: |
|---|---|
| Thirty-three. | Forty-three |

PAULO:  Just joking; thirty-three, thirty-three.

THEO:  I'll be right back. *(exits to kitchen)*

LUISA:  I might as well be fifty-three.  I'm going to grow old all alone.

PAULO:  All of us get to live until we die.

LUISA:  What?

PAULO:  Plus you'll have a child to keep you company.

LUISA:  No I won't.  She'll probably go to Borneo or Tibet or Zimbabwe or somewhere and disappear like you and I'll never see her again.

*(MIRELLA exits to her apartment downstairs.)*

CRISTINA:  *(to PAULO)* Yeah, and it'll all be your fault.

*(THEO returns bearing cake with lit candles.  ALL except Luisa begin to sing.)*

ALL: Happy b -

LUISA: NO STUPID SONG!

THEO: Okay, at least blow out the candles so we don't get wax in the frosting.

*(LUISA starts to blow out candles.)*

PAULO: Make a wish first.

LUISA: I don't need to.

*(As LUISA blows out candles, MIRELLA returns with an object wrapped in tissue.)*

CRISTINA: Why?

LUISA: Because Mirella *(hesitates)* took me to a fortune teller.

BERTHE: I want to go.

THEO: Tell us what she said.

LUISA: I can't tell you that.

CRISTINA: Can you at least say if it's good?

LUISA: It might be.

MIRELLA: This is for you.

*(MIRELLA gives LUISA the tissue-wrapped object. LUISA opens it to reveal hand-knit baby booties. LUISA holds them up.)*

LUISA: Aww.

MIRELLA: My mother, God bless her soul, *(crosses herself)*
she made them.

LUISA: Ohh, are you sure?

MIRELLA: *(shrugs)* This way they will be used.

CRISTINA: *(aside to LUISA, but now half in jest)* Check for needles.

PAULO: Hey, step right up, it's showtime! *(to BERTHE)* You ready?

*(PAULO and BERTHE ready the room for their performance.)*

PAULO: Now remember, this is just a taste of it. This part comes near the end.

CRISTINA: You two really plan to make a living doing this stuff?

PAULO: This "stuff" is art.

CRISTINA: I don't know art from Wal-Mart.

BERTHE: My mother always warned that my dancing was "brotlose Kunst" - art without bread.

LUISA: But you ignored her?

BERTHE: No no, she encouraged me.

THEO: What kind of mother would do that?

BERTHE: A mother who is a painter.

PAULO: Her mother's great. Can we get on with the show?

*(They finish preparing the room.)*

BERTHE: This piece was inspired by Carlo Goldoni.

PAULO: The most amazing playwright ever.

BERTHE: He wrote more than two hundred and fifty plays.

PAULO: Can you imagine? The guy must have pissed ink.

BERTHE: We call this part "Zur Liebe Aufsteigen", "Climbing to Love". *(PAULO gazes adoringly at Berthe, forgetting himself for a moment. Then, snapping out of it -)*

PAULO: Ready? Places.

*(PAULO looks and sees that he and BERTHE are already at places.)*

PAULO: Oh. Well, curtain.

*(Lights fade slowly to a soft golden patina as BERTHE and PAULO perform mime and dance with music. The SCENARIO is that a depressed prince is fashioning rope into a noose with the intention of hanging himself. He sees a beautiful woman dancing above him who does possess the will to live, evidenced by her animated dancing and exotic contortions. This vision makes him reject death. He wants to be with her. He now uses the noose to hook on to something near her. In their actual stage performance the woman would be above the man and he would scale the rope vertically to reach his beloved. In the villa they must perform this action horizontally. He struggles to pull himself toward the woman. He reaches her but is totally exhausted. She admonishes him to get up. He can't. She blows a kiss on him. He rouses slightly. She pulls him to his full height and kisses him. He is now energized. He uses a pen knife to slice the rope open, pulls from it a magical pop-up bouquet and gives it to her. They are in love.)*

*(Applause at end of performance.)*

## ACT 2, SCENE 4

*(Lakeside park, afternoon next day, Friday. The wind has kicked up. CRISTINA, LUISA and PAULO are walking up from the shore. They have had the memorial service and scattered ashes in the lake. THEO, at shoreside with his back to the audience, tarries to reflect and shake out the last ashes from the vase. They start to pack up. The wind complicates the packing. When THEO turns we see that ashes cover his front. His gait is unsteady and he struggles to get ash out of his eye. Others can't help laughing at his awkward and ashen appearance.)*

THEO: Stop it.

LUISA: She's made you into a ghost.

THEO: I don't know how this happens. One day she's laughing in her garden picking tomatoes and the next day I'm holding a vase with two pints of dust. *(turns empty vase upside down)* How does this happen?

CRISTINA: We need to get a move on. It looks like it might rain.

THEO: Wait a minute. There's one more thing. *(picks up bag)* I thought it would be nice to give each of you girls a piece of Momma's jewelry. You too Berthe, she'd want you to have something too.

CRISTINA: That's nice but I think there's a fairness issue at stake here.

PAULO: *(perturbed)* Come on.

CRISTINA: No; Luisa. *(makes looping gesture on her neck to represent necklace)* Remember?

THEO: *(annoyed)*
Oh Cristina.

CRISTINA: What do you mean, "Oh Cristina"? She already helped herself to Momma's jewelry.

LUISA: I told you what happened!

CRISTINA: I don't think so. Whenever Momma made cake she was always so careful to cut the pieces equal so there'd be no squabble.

LUISA: That's not how I remember things.

CRISTINA: What family did you grow up in? *(to THEO)* That necklace has diamonds.

PAULO: And a coating of ash, don't forget.

CRISTINA: Do you really want to get in the middle of this?

THEO: Can we please try to remember what the occasion is?

LUISA: You can be such a witch.

CRISTINA: Better a witch than a thief.

LUISA: I did not take anything. *(turns on PAULO)* What do you think, Paulo?

PAULO: Berthe and I could care less about Momma's jewelry.

BERTHE: Umm, can I look first?

THEO: Do you realize how disappointed Momma would be with you? I should put diapers - [on all of you]

*(PAULO sees POLICEMAN approaching, carrying a small cooler.)*

PAULO: Uh-umm, diapers will have to wait. We have a visitor.

*(ALL look.)*

CRISTINA: Oh god, what does he want this time?

LUISA: And how does he keep finding us? Quick, hide the vase. *(grabs and hides it)*

THEO: What are you doing?

LUISA: Jail! We probably just broke the law.

THEO: That is so ri -

POLICEMAN: Whew. I've been looking all over for you.

LUISA: *(blurts)* We didn't know any better.

THEO: Luisa!

POLICEMAN: I think that such a beautiful girl should not worry so much.

LUISA: Oh.

POLICEMAN: *(noticing Theo covered with ashes)* You are all right?

THEO: Oh, yes, some - powder, I spilled some powder, it's nothing.

POLICEMAN: *(to CRISTINA)* You will not believe this but we need your, umm, competenze particolari one more time.

CRISTINA: What "competenze"? All I did was tell you to make a lot of noise and drive fast.

POLICEMAN: That poor man . . .

THEO: Was he okay?

POLICEMAN: He is okay now, yes.

PAULO: Everything finally fell into place?

*(PAULO mimes by dropping his arm. His humor is not appreciated.)*

POLICEMAN: Yes, but his wife, she kicks him out the door. *(does a small kick)*

LUISA: Really? After he went to such great lengths for her.

POLICEMAN: Si. She knew the blue pill was not for her. But today we have a different problem. A man has been missing for one week.

LUISA: But you said you have no crime in Bellano.

POLICEMAN: This man lives outside town.

LUISA: Oh.

POLICEMAN: He and his wife have a history of knocking each other around. You know –

*(POLICEMAN performs extended pantomine of slapping, kicking, shoving. OTHERS look on mesmerized.)*

POLICEMAN: Anyway, his brother reports him missing and he tells me the wife may have something to do with it, if you see what I mean. So I visit and things do not feel right. When you do what I do for a time, you get a feeling for these things.

LUISA: I'm sure.

CRISTINA: Even with no crime.

POLICEMAN: On the floor by the bed I see what looks like blood and in the frigorifero I find salami but I ask "Why is blood all over it." And all the wife says is "Go ask his girlfriends." Her eyes, they wander everywhere *(mimes)* but they always come back to the frigorifero. Strange, no? So I think, "I will bring this to la bella dottoressa; she will know."

*(POLICEMAN reaches into cooler and holds up a plastic evidence bag.)*

THEO: Oh god -

*(THEO, LUISA and BERTHE avert their eyes.)*

LUISA: Yukkk! No! I can't look!

BERTHE: Nein! Ughh! Bitte.

*(POLICEMAN returns bag to cooler.)*

PAULO: If that's what I think it is his name wasn't Longfellow.

*(PAULO's humor confuses POLICEMAN and annoys CRISTINA, THEO and LUISA.)*

LUISA: You are disgusting.

CRISTINA: She's right, you really are.

PAULO: So dump spaghetti on my head.

POLICEMAN: *(to CRISTINA)* I am sorry. Please can you examine this?

CRISTINA: Did you find any other evidence?

THEO: People don't really do that sort of thing.

POLICEMAN: *(pulls from cooler a second evidence bag)* This is in frigorifero also. Almost like meatballs, no?

PAULO: Maybe from Sweden?

THEO: *(annoyed with PAULO)* Enough.

LUISA: *(wincing)* Please put those back.

POLICEMAN: I hope you can identify this too.

CRISTINA: That is not what I do.

POLICEMAN: It is not what I do either. I was trained for smugglers, drugs and tax-cheaters, not this. Please.
*(holds up evidence bag again)*

LUISA: *(grimacing)* Ughh!

*(POLICEMAN returns bag to cooler.)*

BERTHE: Vielen Dank!

*(CRISTINA hobbles to the cooler. POLICEMAN gives her surgical gloves which she puts on.)*

PAULO: Decapitations must be so much easier to identify.

LUISA: Cristina, how can you do that!?

*(CRISTINA examines the bags; holds her nose.)*

CRISTINA: These I think are mozarella balls that have been in the fridge way too long. But this, *(shakes her head)* maybe your theory is not so crazy.

POLICEMAN:  So you think -

CRISTINA:  I think you have good reason to bring the wife in for questioning. My guess is her husband will never speak to his brother again.

PAULO:  That's not the only thing he'll never do again.

POLICEMAN:  *(puts lid on cooler and starts to leave)*
I knew la bella dottoressa can help.  Thank you so much.  I must hurry now.  Oh, have there been any more problems with the . . different drawings from your book?

CRISTINA:  No, they seem to be okay.

POLICEMAN:  Well, if there is anything our humble police department can do for you during the rest of your visit, please, just call me.

*(POLICEMAN gives CRISTINA his card.  Their hands touch and briefly linger.)*

POLICEMAN:  For you too.  *(gives LUISA a card)*

CRISTINA:  *(clasping his card to her chest)* Umm, tomorrow night, it's our last night, and we're having a sort of farewell dinner.  If you're not on duty or anything, we'd love to have you join us.

LUISA:  I'm cooking something special.

POLICEMAN:  That is a very nice offer but my mother always cooks dinner for me on Saturday.
*(makes delicious food gesture of fingers to lips)*

CRISTINA:  Her recipe is from our Italian mother.

POLICEMAN:  Hmmm . . . I think your meal is a very special event.  I will try to come.  Grazie.

LUISA:  Good.

CRISTINA:  Yes good.

## ACT 2, SCENE 5

*(Evening, Saturday. ALL sit at dining table, finishing the main course. An empty chair is next to CRISTINA. A fair amount of wine has been enjoyed. MIRELLA and LUISA will soon start clearing dishes and serving coffee and dessert.)*

THEO: Lu, I don't think Momma would be offended, in fact just the opposite, if I said that was the best pumpkin gnocchi I ever had.

PAULO: I never order it in a restaurant because I'll always be disappointed. But this, this was - *(kisses his joined thumb and finger)*

LUISA: I maybe should have used more sage. Anyway, I couldn't have done it without Mirella.

MIRELLA: Nonsenso, I just turn on oven.

LUISA: Right.

BERTHE: And the table - so beautiful.

CRISTINA: *(a mild tease)* The dishes were arranged so - perfectly.

*(THEO is in on the tease. LUISA flashes anger. OTHERS are confused but let it go.)*

THEO: The only thing missing is our friendly neighborhood poliziotto.

CRISTINA: The one time we expect him to show, he doesn't. Men.

PAULO: Everybody may be leaving tomorrow, but guess what - we'll be back in the summer! The producer called and he's booked us for three weeks in Rome and if that goes well he needs acts for Venice, Florence and Milan in the fall. We're off and running!

BERTHE: Do not get removed yet.

PAULO: I think you mean "carried away", and I'm not. *(he clearly is)*

BERTHE: Yes you are, darling.

CRISTINA:  Darling?

BERTHE:  I learn from American movies.

PAULO:  Thank you, darling.

*(Knocks at the door. THEO opens door. It is the POLICEMAN.)*

THEO:  Hello.  I'm dressed this time.

POLICEMAN:  Thank you.  I leave handcuffs at home.  I must apologize.  A car hit a cow and I had to stop a fight between the farmer and driver.

CRISTINA:  Oh.  We hope everything is okay.

POLICEMAN:  Except for the cow.  I hope I am not too late.

LUISA:  We saved some gnocchi just in case.

CRISTINA:  *(a little bashful, gestures to the empty chair beside her)* Here, we saved a seat too.

*(He sits.  LUISA serves him.)*

CRISTINA:  Wine?

POLICEMAN:  Si.  This is very special - I do not always dine with four beautiful signoras.

*(CRISTINA fills his wine glass.  Conversation stops as ALL watch POLICEMAN relish the meal.)*

POLICEMAN:  This is almost as fine as Momma's. *(noticing LUISA's disappointment)* No, no, that is very great praise.

LUISA:  Thank you. . . Is everyone else ready for dessert?  We have a surprise for you.  Something really special.

CRISTINA:  I'll get the coffee.

LUISA: No, I will. Just relax.

CRISTINA: I can help. I'll get it.

LUISA: I said I have it handled. Sit. Please.

CRISTINA: Yes, darling.

LUISA: That's better.

THEO: Don't you girls get started.

*(LUISA and MIRELLA take up used plates and exit to kitchen.)*

CRISTINA: Mirella says we need to be out by noon, or else.

PAULO: Oh, she's all meow and no scratch.

CRISTINA: Maybe for you.

POLICEMAN: This is so very good.

CRISTINA: We're glad you like it.

*(LUISA and MIRELLA enter with dessert and coffee.)*

THEO: Who comes tomorrow, Mirella?

MIRELLA: Russians. They are as bad as Americans.

THEO: You used to think Americans were worse.

MIRELLA: *(with good humor)* Only some of them.

*(LUISA and MIRELLA serve canolli and coffee. As MIRELLA serves THEO she lingers, placing a hand on his shoulder for more than a moment. He looks at her. She tousles his hair. They exchange a smile. One covered plate is saved for last. LUISA approaches CRISTINA.)*

LUISA: I finally convinced Mirella that your work is not X-rated.

MIRELLA: So we made you a -

*(MIRELLA consults LUISA for right word.)*

MIRELLA: "peace offering".

LUISA: A really big piece. Ta-da!

*(With a flourish, LUISA reveals a very large, very phallic canolli with extra filling. ALL laugh except CRISTINA who is embarrassed, then perturbed, but she quickly joins in the amusement.)*

CRISTINA: Okay, okay.

PAULO: *(mimicking POLICEMAN)* Oh signora scientist, can you please help us identify this?

*(ALL laugh, the POLICEMAN most heartily.)*

LUISA: She is the expert.

CRISTINA: I don't know; this may be too much for one woman.

BERTHE: I can help.

*(More laughter. CRISTINA retrieves manuscript nearby. The boot-cast is gone but she moves gingerly because of her back.)*

CRISTINA: All right everybody, I have a surprise too. Do you know what this is?

THEO: You did it!

CRISTINA: Yes, I did it. I am flying home with a sore back, a healed foot, and one completed manuscript! Which means I will meet my deadline, which means I just might keep my job and maybe even become associate professor with tenure.

PAULO: Congratulations, Sis. Really.

CRISTINA:  Now, every day this fall I want you to check the New York Times so that you know when
*(mock-announcer voice, looking at MS cover)*
"Variation in Zygote Formation Strategies Among Vertebrates" reaches the best-sellers list.

THEO:  The Times it is.

CRISTINA:  You'll find it in non-fiction.

THEO:  I want to show you kids something your mother kept.

*(THEO gets a nearby box and removes a hand-made origami fortune-telling children's game. MIRELLA is immediately interested in it.)*

THEO:  Remember this?

*(THEO hands game to CRISTINA.)*

CRISTINA:  Yes!  Momma used to make them.

LUISA:  We all loved to play.

*(CRISTINA tries to work game but can't quite remember how it goes.)*

THEO:  Careful, it's a little fragile.

LUISA:  Here, I'll show you.

*(LUISA takes the game and, using both hands, operates it properly.)*

PAULO:  Let's play.

LUISA:  I already had my fortune told, remember?

MIRELLA:  May I see?

*(LUISA hands game to MIRELLA who quickly examines it as OTHERS continue talking. MIRELLA puffs a quick subtle breath on it.)*

PAULO:  Well this could be a back-up.

CRISTINA:  Maybe it will expand our futures.

LUISA:  *(holds her belly)* Mine is expanding plenty already, thank you very much.

BERTHE:  We play this in Germany too.  We call it Nasenkneifer.

LUISA:  What's that?

BERTHE:  Here, I show you.

*(MIRELLA hands game to BERTHE, who inserts fingers and moves it toward PAULO's face.)*

BERTHE:  Nose pincher.

*(Laughter.)*

POLICEMAN:  We play in Italia too.

PAULO:  Come on, Lu.

LUISA:  Okay. *(takes game from BERTHE)* Berthe, you be first.

BERTHE:  No, I think this is special between you and your Momma.

LUISA:  Really?  Okay, Paulo, pick a color.

PAULO:  Blue.

LUISA:  *(operates game)* B-L-U-E.  Now pick a number.

PAULO:  Four.

LUISA:  One-two-three-four.  Now pick another number.

PAULO:  Three.

LUISA
*(lifts the "3" corner and reads)* "Your creativity can breathe life into dust."

CRISTINA: What the - [heck?]

THEO: His mind is the only one here that could possibly understand that.

BERTHE: I agree with you.

*(But PAULO is as perplexed as OTHERS.)*

LUISA: *(to CRISTINA)* All right, your turn. Pick a color.

CRISTINA: Pink.

LUISA: P-I-N-K. And a number.

CRISTINA: Three.

LUISA: One-two-three. And one of those.

CRISTINA: Two.

LUISA: *(lifts a corner)* "Beware the sharp mind that dulls the heart."

CRISTINA: Oh. *(glances at POLICEMAN)* I think someone's heart has been sharpened lately.

PAULO: Oh really, darling?

LUISA: I think so. Okay my turn, I guess. I'm not sure I want to do this.

PAULO: You have to; we did.

*(LUISA hands game to CRISTINA.)*

CRISTINA: Okay, a color.

LUISA: Green.

CRISTINA: G-R-E-E-N. And a number?

LUISA: Lucky seven.

CRISTINA: One-two-three-four-five-six-seven. Another one.

LUISA: Four.

CRISTINA: *(lifts a corner)* "You will travel somewhere new."

LUISA: Oh my.

BERTHE: Is that what the fortune teller said?

*(LUISA and MIRELLA exchange a knowing glance.)*

LUISA: It's close.

THEO: More travel, huh?

*(LUISA gives a noncommittal shrug.)*

THEO: It feels like Momma's with us.

LUISA: At least not like completely gone. *(to POLICEMAN)* Our mother died last winter.

POLICEMAN: I am sorry.

THEO: *(to LUISA)* Have you started to pack yet?

LUISA: *(hesitates)* No.

THEO: Me neither. You're sure you're okay to fly?

LUISA: *(hesitates again)* Yes, for a while longer.

CRISTINA: *(to POLICEMAN)* She's having a baby.

POLICEMAN: Really? Congratulations.

THEO: My first grandchild.

PAULO: Ummm, granddaughter.

THEO: Yes, I know, granddaughter.

PAULO: But . . . not your first grandchild.

THEO: What do you mean?

PAULO: Well, I wasn't sure when to tell you but you already have a grandson.

THEO: Berthe!

BERTHE: Do not look at me.

PAULO: No, not her. I had a girlfriend before Berthe and now I have a son, Aldric. He's five. He lives in Munich, with his mother. The woman who got migraines from my maturity.

CRISTINA: You already have a child?

LUISA: Really? I have a nephew? Here, in Europe?

PAULO: Well he's not in Tibet. He's a great kid and I'm trying to be a decent father now. I want him to meet all of you.

THEO: Sooner the better. And pictures, I want pictures!

PAULO: Definitely. You'll see he has Momma's nose. Umm . . . Berthe and I have some more news - we have decided . . .

BERTHE: To marry! Uns zu verbinden!

THEO: That's great! Just great, great news.

BERTHE: Wish me luck.

CRISTINA: Aww, congratulations.

LUISA: Fantastic! That's really fantastic, Paulo.

POLICEMAN: Si, felicitazioni.

THEO: I always wanted a contortionist in the family.

PAULO: It seems that after meeting all of you, she decided I was okay.

BERTHE: Because I saw that none of you are as crazy as him.

CRISTINA: Wait 'til you get to know us better.

THEO: *(to PAULO)* When?

PAULO: Sometime this summer or fall.

THEO: I have to write it down.

BERTHE: We have not told my parents yet.

THEO: What will they think?

BERTHE: They will be happy. They really like Paulo. I don't understand it.

PAULO: We wanted you to know before you flew home.

LUISA: *(to THEO)* Yeah, about that, I was wondering . . . are our plane tickets refundable?

THEO: No, I don't think so. Why?

*(Beat.)*

LUISA: Well, because I have some news too. Don't worry, it's not a bomb, well, maybe a cherry bomb *(indicates smallness with fingers)* but not a, you know . . .

THEO: *(anxious and losing patience)* Luisa.

LUISA: What? Okay. It's just that, well, it's like Momma's fortune game just said: I'm travelling someplace new, right? Well, I'm already there. I've decided to stay here, in Italy, and have my baby here.

THEO: What?!

LUISA: I'm going to name her Sonia Giovanni and raise her here, right where Momma grew up.

THEO: You can't do that!

LUISA: Why not!? Didn't you tell me to take charge of my life?

THEO: Not this way! This is nuts! Not to mention dumb and really really stupid.

LUISA: I don't think Momma would think so. I think she would like it. Look how good she turned out.

THEO: That wasn't because she grew up in Bellano.

MIRELLA: How do you know this?

LUISA: Didn't Momma make exactly this sort of decision when she was young and moved to America?

THEO: Yeah, but you're not so really young.

LUISA: What am I, like really ancient?

THEO: No, I mean -

CRISTINA: *(to THEO)* Don't go there. *(to LUISA)* But you are pregnant.

THEO: And you're alone. Where do you think you and - Sonia - are going to live?

LUISA: Mirella has offered me the room her husband had downstairs.

CRISTINA: You and Mirella?! Okay, now I have to side with you Dad, you have gone completely nuts.

LUISA: No I haven't. We've talked about it and this can work.

MIRELLA: A big appartamento is downstairs with big empty room. A baby will make it not so empty.

THEO: I appreciate your kindness but this is a completely hare-brained idea.

MIRELLA: What is hare-brain?

(CRISTINA *points to her brain and with fingers indicates tiny.*)

THEO: What are you going to live on?

LUISA: Maybe I can teach.

THEO: What can you teach?

LUISA: I don't know. "Depression as a Second Language"? "Contemporary Designs in Table Settings."

THEO: Are you taking medication?

PAULO: I think her plan makes sense. It's not like she's winning the lottery in Seattle.

CRISTINA: This from the brother with the disappearing act whose life was so well planned?

PAULO: No, I really do. The only way to know where a line is, is to cross it.

THEO: Will you stop that?

CRISTINA: *(to POLICEMAN)* Our brother thinks he's Socrates.

POLICEMAN: Ahh.

CRISTINA: *(to PAULO)* This is an ocean she's crossing, not some line. And your logic stinks.

PAULO: No it doesn't. I think she's being brave. Kind of like Joan of Arc, but in Italy not France. You go Sis!

MIRELLA: This region has many handsome men. Many single, handsome men.

POLICEMAN: *(puffs himself up)* E vero.

CRISTINA: Si, e vero. Throw me in the pot and turn on the heat.

LUISA: Cristina!

BERTHE: Can I stay too?

PAULO: You're getting married, Fraulein.

MIRELLA: And no crime. And no mice.

THEO: *(to LUISA)* What about your job?

LUISA: Let me see: eight to five in a cubicle with no windows and rain half the year - Italian villa on Lake Como. It's a tough call, Dad.

BERTHE: Paulo and I will not be far away. Maybe she can help our new company.

LUISA: *(with uncharacteristic assertiveness)* Listen, all of you. I'm serious about this. I am not going with you tomorrow. And I do not need anyone's approval.

*(A beat.)*

THEO: Well, what does an old man know who can't even walk straight? *(to MIRELLA)* You're sure you're okay with this?

MIRELLA: Ehh, the Giovannis come from here. It is una superba idea!

THEO: *(conceding)* You are thirty-three.

LUISA: You remember!

THEO: I wrote it down. *(starting to feel sad)* So when's the due date?

LUISA: Mid-August.

MIRELLA: *(to THEO)* Maybe you could visit then.

POLICEMAN: *(to CRISTINA)* Can you come too?

CRISTINA: Classes don't start 'til September.

THEO: Well, okay.

MIRELLA: Bravo, bravo! *(gives THEO a pat on the butt, surprising ALL)*

LUISA: *(to THEO)* Will you be sure to water the tomatoes?

THEO: What?

LUISA: The tomatoes I planted last week. Remember?

THEO: Oh, sure, okay. I better write that down.

LUISA: Don't forget.

THEO: What I won't forget is that I'm the only one left in Seattle.

CRISTINA: Oh quit it. I'll come visit more often.

*(Positions now are: PAULO and BERTHE stand together; CRISTINA and POLICE-MAN stand together; THEO, LUISA and MIRELLA stand together with THEO in the middle.)*

PAULO: Maybe we can plan our wedding for August.

LUISA: We can meet Aldric.

PAULO: And he can meet Sonia.

CRISTINA:  His cousin.

LUISA:  Your niece.

THEO:  My grandchildren.

POLICEMAN:  La familia.

BERTHE:  *(raises a glass)* Auf die Zukunft.

MIRELLA:  *(raises a glass)* Il futuro.

LUISA:  *(raises a glass)* The future - welcome.

*(As lights slowly fade, LUISA takes a sip of wine.  CRISTINA takes glass from LUISA and sips while gently wagging a finger at her.  Somewhere MOMMA is smiling at her united family.)*

END OF PLAY

## TRANSLATION NOTES

1.1. Comé? - What?

1.3. Hello Hans. Yes, I'm in Bellano, on Lake Como. . . Shit. . . But we had an agreement. . . Okay. . . Does Berthe know? . . . Yes, let me tell her. . . Okay. . . Goodbye.

1.3. This is Mirella at Signor Gozzi villa. Criminals are here. [and] No, not you. I need you here, pronto. Yes, yes. Pronto. Thank you.

1.3. Per favore. - Please

1.3. Sei nicht albern. - Don't be silly.

2.1. Klasse. - Excellent.

2.2. Buona sera. - Good evening.

2.2. Ja, eine winzige Maus. - Yeah, a little mouse.

2.2. Hallo. Na, rate mal, wer ich bin. - Hello. Guess who this is. Hab dich lieb. Seh dich bald. - I love you. See you soon.

2.2. Schrei mich nicht so an! - Don't yell at me!

2.2. Sie still! - Shut up!

2.4. Vielen Dank. - Thank you very much.

2.5. Uns zu verbinden. - We are tying the knot.

2.5. E vero. - It is true.

# The Thing With Feathers

a play by

## DUANE KELLY

*"Caelum non animum mutant qui trans mare currunt."*
–Horace
*"Those who run across the sea change the sky but not their soul."*

# CHARACTERS

HARRY HOWELL, 53, expat American; has one below-the-knee prosthetic leg; smokes cigarettes

LOAN, Vietnamese, adult, age indeterminate (pronounced low-awn with accent on awn; Loan means phoenix in Vietnamese)

JAVIER, 17, Harry's adopted son

DORA, 37, Costa Rican, farm's bookkeeper and Harry's common-law wife

CLARE, 31, American

CARLOS, 40s, Costa Rican coffee farmer

RIMBAUD, parrot with large vocabulary (name spoken with French pronunciation - ram-bow with the accent on bow; however the echo of Rambo, the Stallone movie character, is intentional)

# TIME

December 2000

# PLACE

A large well-worn office on a mid-sized coffee farm in the central valley of Costa Rica. Office is within the residence of the farm's owner/manager. Essentials are window with a view onto the farm, desk with drawers, couch large enough for sleeping, TV, cupboard containing liquor, file cabinets, globe that spins. Desk top is in disarray with piles of files and paper. Books are about. There could be a veranda opening off the office. A largish bird cage contains Rimbaud, a verbose parrot.

# *ACT* 1

## SCENE 1

*(Pre-dawn, Tuesday, December 2000. Light rain falls outside. A cock crows in the distance. A futbol game plays on TV at low volume. LOAN observes scene. HARRY sleeps fitfully on couch where he had collapsed from fatigue, worry and vodka. A light blanket covers Harry, arranged so it is not apparent that he has a prosthetic leg. Partially empty vodka bottle nearby. JAVIER enters, observes scene dejectedly. He has seen Harry in this condition too often lately. LOAN is invisible to Javier. HARRY is tossing, having a nightmare. LOAN approaches couch and makes a motion over HARRY's head; he becomes more agitated, which doesn't displease her. She makes another motion and HARRY becomes still; she has dispelled his nightmare. JAVIER replaces cap on vodka bottle, puts it away and gets a second light blanket. As he walks back toward HARRY the futbol game distracts him. When score is announced he is disappointed. Turns off TV, puts blanket over HARRY. Notices Harry's prosthetic leg on floor, unseen by audience until now, picks it up and examines it, leans it against furniture so that Harry can easily reach it when he wakes.)*

RIMBAUD THE PARROT:  I saw the best -

JAVIER:  Shh!

RIMBAUD THE PARROT:  - minds of my generation.

JAVIER:  Shh!

RIMBAUD THE PARROT:  Destroyed by madness.

JAVIER:  Shhh.

RIMBAUD THE PARROT:  The best minds -

*(HARRY starts to rouse. JAVIER notices.)*

RIMBAUD THE PARROT: - destroyed by madness.

JAVIER: Shhhh!

*(JAVIER pulls water pistol from desk drawer.)*

RIMBAUD THE PARROT: Madness, madness, madness.

*(JAVIER squirts RIMBAUD.)*

RIMBAUD THE PARROT: Squawk.

*(RIMBAUD is finally silent. In the fashion of a boy playing, JAVIER blows pretend smoke off muzzle of squirt gun. Replaces in drawer. HARRY stops rousing, returns to sleep.)*

## ACT 1, SCENE 2

*(Later that Tuesday morning. HARRY sits on couch, cup of coffee at hand. DORA at desk, JAVIER getting ready to go to school, has his small backpack ready and is now looking for the net bag containing his futbol gear.)*

DORA: Lucia gave birth last night in the barn, but her kid was stillborn.

HARRY: Good, one less goat to chew on coffee leaves.

JAVIER: Is Lucia all right?

DORA: She seems to be.

HARRY: But the barn's not.

DORA: Yeah, you've got a small lake in there from the roof.

HARRY: It's not supposed to rain in December. *(to JAVIER)* What are you looking for?

JAVIER: (finds net bag) Here it is.

HARRY: You're going to be late for school.

JAVIER: I'll be late getting home tonight. Futbol practice.

HARRY: You do have school this morning.

JAVIER: I know. I was wondering if you could help me with something.

(*JAVIER pulls from his bag an athletic shoe that's mangled and caked with mud.*)

DORA: That's a pretty shoe.

JAVIER: Manuel's two dogs were fighting over it last night, like some bone.

DORA: A bone would be in better shape.

HARRY: How'd two dogs end up with that?

JAVIER: Manuel threw it to them.

HARRY: What?

JAVIER: We were all teasing him because he let two goals score in the last five minutes. He got mad and started throwing our shoes across the field. The dogs picked mine for dinner.

DORA: We can see that.

HARRY: Javi, how'd you let him do that?

JAVIER: He grabbed it before I could stop him. This is ruined now; so I was wondering -

HARRY: No.

JAVIER: - if you could maybe -

HARRY: Forget it.

JAVIER: help me get a new pair.

HARRY: Do you know how many beans I need to harvest to pay for new shoes?

DORA: Harry, don't.

HARRY: Don't what?

DORA: You know what.

HARRY: No I don't.

DORA: Be like that.

HARRY: *(to DORA)* I'll be whatever I want to be. *(to JAVIER)* It's a damn lot of beans.

JAVIER: We've got the playoffs next month.

DORA: I have some money.

HARRY: You do? Well good, 'cause I don't.

DORA: But you're not going to get new shoes before tonight. Don't you have an old pair?

JAVIER: They don't fit.

HARRY: Let me see.

*(JAVIER hands HARRY the shoe.)*

HARRY: *(smelling)* Whew! His dogs chew better than they smell. Use duct tape. In the tool shop. That'll work. Knock some of the mud off first.

JAVIER: It'd be in even worse shape except this cat showed up and the dogs decided she'd taste even better.

HARRY:  She had to smell better.

DORA:  Maybe I can take you into San Jose this weekend and we'll look at shoes.

HARRY:  And you tell your friend Manuel -

JAVIER:  He's not really my friend -

HARRY:  that if anything like this happens again you'll take his dogs and throw -

JAVIER:  Umm, have you ever seen his dogs?

HARRY:  Tell him they'll come out looking worse than this.

*(HARRY returns shoe.)*

JAVIER:  They're really big dogs.

HARRY:  I don't care.

JAVIER:  With really big teeth.

HARRY:  Go on -

JAVIER:  That go grrrrrr -

HARRY:  Get your butt to school.

JAVIER:  Will you go to the playoffs?

HARRY:  Go to school.  Hurry, while the rain's stopped.

DORA:  Of course he will; we'll both be there.  I'll save you some dinner tonight.

*(JAVIER exits.)*

DORA:  We need to come up with a plan.

HARRY:  Go ahead, take him shopping.

DORA: You know what I mean.

HARRY: I don't have time.

DORA: That's more or less the problem.  The bank wants it by next Friday.

HARRY: I'm well aware.

DORA: They're not going to give another extension.  And -

HARRY: I know. . . . How far behind am I, four months?

DORA: Five.

HARRY: Shit.  And how much cash do we have?

DORA: Enough for two more weeks.

HARRY: That's it?

DORA: Maybe three weeks; but yeah, that's it.

*(DORA picks up glass, sniffs.)*

DORA: Where's the bottle?

*(HARRY is confused because bottle is gone.)*

DORA: This isn't good.

HARRY: Farming sucks right now. . . . What, you haven't noticed?

DORA: You're drinking way too much.

HARRY: *(holds up cup)* Coffee?

DORA: You're not taking care of yourself.  You have a scab on your stump.  You don't come to bed.

HARRY: So the farm's okay but I'm not.

DORA: Losing the farm's one thing - boy have you been one big cup of pain in the ass?

HARRY: Lay off.

DORA: No, that's what you need to do. Lay off this. And quit riding Javier. Sure we're in bad shape -

HARRY: You don't know the half of it.

DORA: But drowning in this doesn't -

HARRY: I told you, lay off!

(*HARRY makes a threatening gesture.*)

DORA: Go ahead! What is wrong with you?

HARRY: Just lay off. . . I haven't been so well lately.

DORA: Oh really?! . . . How not so well?

HARRY: Hard to say.

DORA: You need to figure out how to say.

HARRY: There's these ants, they keep running out, skittering every which way.

DORA: Ants?

HARRY: Ants.

DORA: What kind of ants?

HARRY: Up here. (*points to his head*) Black, brown, red, big, tiny, fast and faster, scitter here, scutter there, go go go. I slam on the brake but it's like the gas. Just go faster. Barn leaks, need money for university, tractor brakes shot, fail at this, fail at that.

DORA:  Harry, Harry, Harry -

HARRY:  When I figure it out -

DORA:  You're not alone here.

HARRY:  I'll figure it out.

DORA:  Maybe we should just leave?

HARRY:  Who?

DORA:  Me and Javi, that's who.

HARRY:  Javi will be gone next fall anyway.

DORA:  If there's money for school.  He may have to wait a year or -

HARRY:  No!, I'll find the money.

DORA:  We can leave you and the goats to run the place.

HARRY:  I could sell part of the farm.

DORA:  You're not serious?

HARRY:  I could sell the south forty.

DORA:  That'd be like . . .

HARRY:  What?

DORA:  Cutting off a leg.

HARRY:  Sometimes that can save the patient.

DORA:  And what about when the price comes back?  You'll regret it.

HARRY:  You're optimistic today.

DORA:  No, not really.

HARRY:  Well that's the best I've been able to come up with.  That or bankruptcy.

DORA:  Who'd buy now?  Every farmer in the valley is like us or worse.

HARRY:  You never know.  At least I could ask around.

DORA:  I feel like I don't know you anymore.

*(Doorbell rings.)*

HARRY:  Join the crowd.

DORA:  I've got to get that.

*(DORA exits.  LOAN enters.  HARRY is afraid of her.  DORA returns.  LOAN is invisible to DORA.)*

DORA:  You have a visitor,

*(HARRY looks at LOAN.)*

DORA:  *(off HARRY's look in the wrong direction)* out there, someone from the States.

HARRY:  From the States?  You sure?

DORA:  Well I didn't ask for I.D.  You have a visitor, at the front door, from the U.S., probably.

*(HARRY glances at LOAN.)*

HARRY:  Oh.  At the front door.  What does she want?

DORA:  How'd you know she was a she?

HARRY:  I don't know; how did you?

DORA: Gee Harry, I saw her!

HARRY: Where?

DORA: At the front door! Her. She's a she.

HARRY: Oh.

DORA: A young she, kind of. Says she's doing research, research about coffee. Says she wrote you a letter. That's what she says.

HARRY: Great.

DORA: What do I know? Want me to send her away or have her come in?

HARRY: I don't know.

DORA: I'll bring her in.

*(DORA exits. HARRY remains afraid of LOAN. DORA returns with CLARE.)*

DORA: This is Harry Howell. It's his farm.

CLARE: A boy on a bicycle told me this was the right place. He was loaded down with soccer balls and books.

HARRY: Yes, he would have told you that. And this is Dora. She runs the farm, and me.

CLARE: Oh. Nice to meet you both. I'm Clare . . . Gutterman.

DORA: No one runs him. Nice to meet you.

CLARE: Sorry to barge in like this. Do you know who I am? I mean, do you know about me?

DORA: Uh, are you famous or something?

CLARE: No, hardly.

HARRY:  Should we?

CLARE:  Well, I wrote you a letter, a couple of weeks ago.

*(HARRY looks at his messy desk.)*

HARRY:  I never saw it.  The mail is slow here.

CLARE:  I'm writing a thesis about the coffee industry.  I'm finishing up an MBA program at Columbia, that's in -

HARRY:  I know where Columbia is.

CLARE:  I don't mean the country.

HARRY:  Neither do I.

CLARE:  Okay.  And this thesis . . . You look so worried; I don't want to move in or anything.

HARRY:  That's the best news we've had all morning.  Could you have picked a more depressing topic?

CLARE:  Actually it's fascinating.

HARRY:  Not if you're a farmer.

CLARE:  I've really barged in on you, I know.

DORA:  It's all right.

HARRY:  It is?

DORA:  We had just finished.

*(DORA arranges accounting papers and starts to exit.  CLARE retrieves from a bag a notebook marked "Columbia University".)*

HARRY: *(to DORA)* There should be fourteen pickers today. Armando knows where I want them.

DORA: Okay.

*(DORA exits.)*

CLARE: This thesis, it's like the last thing I need to graduate. . . . I've been trying to call but no one answers.

*(HARRY picks up phone to test it.)*

HARRY: Still down. Supposed to be fixed yesterday. And then what?

CLARE: After it's fixed?

HARRY: After you graduate. From not the country.

CLARE: Well, Starbucks has offered me a job in Seattle, at their headquarters.

HARRY: Hmm, Starbucks buys a lot of my coffee.

CLARE: Maybe they'll buy even more after my thesis. They say they want all their executives to read it.

HARRY: So how'd you end up here?

CLARE: Well Costa Rica was -

HARRY: No, here, here at my farm. Which seems to be a popular destination. Where you're not moving in or anything.

CLARE: Starbucks gave me addresses of farms. But no phone numbers or emails.

HARRY: But you were calling.

CLARE: From the co-op, they gave me your number at the co-op. They said I should interview you. They said you were the expert.

HARRY:  That's why I'm so successful.

CLARE:  I really think they felt sorry for me because my Spanish is non-existent.

*(LOAN exits.  HARRY notices.)*

RIMBAUD THE PARROT:  The women come and go.

HARRY:  They certainly do.

CLARE:  What?

RIMBAUD THE PARROT:  Talking of Michelangelo.

CLARE:  Oh I didn't see him.

HARRY:  That's Rimbaud.  Just -

RIMBAUD THE PARROT:  The women come and go.

HARRY:  *(over)* Ignore him.

RIMBAUD THE PARROT:  Talking of Michelangelo -

HARRY:  *(over)* That's enough!

*(HARRY opens desk drawer and removes squirt gun.  CLARE flinches.  HARRY squirts RIMBAUD.)*

RIMBAUD THE PARROT:  Squawk.

HARRY:  *(to CLARE)* What did you think I was going to do with it?

RIMBAUD THE PARROT:  Squawk.

*(HARRY returns gun to drawer.)*

HARRY:  You were saying?

CLARE:  And because you're American.

HARRY:  What?

CLARE:  Why they gave me -

HARRY:  Not.

CLARE:  Not?

HARRY:  Not American.

CLARE:  But -

HARRY:  Costa Rican.  My passport says Costa Rica.

CLARE:  Then because you were American.  You were, right, weren't you?  They said you were.  Anyway because you speak good English, they thought I'd get more information.

HARRY:  I see.  Well the truth is they're bastards who won't tell you anything about their own farms.

CLARE:  You think so?  Didn't seem that way.  They also gave me the name of *(checks in her notebook)* Carlos Alvarado.  Said he has a big farm and speaks English so I plan to go there too.  Do you maybe have fifteen or so minutes now?

HARRY:  Not really, not this morning.

CLARE:  I've come a long way.

HARRY:  We all have.

CLARE:  Please?

*(Beat.)*

HARRY:  Just a few minutes.

CLARE:  Thanks.  So can you give me your take on why farmers are having such a rough time?

HARRY:  Three words:  price of coffee.  Four years ago we were getting two dollars a pound for green beans.  Times were good.  Now the price is barely fifty cents.  You don't need your MBA to figure out that when you spend more to grow a crop than it sells for, that's a sick business.

CLARE:  Have any farms gone under?

HARRY:  Two or three.  There'll be more.  We have a saying down here: Coffee gives you a hat but steals your shirt.  Right now we're all just about butt naked and that's not a pretty sight.

CLARE:  No.  How long have you lived here?

HARRY:  Thirty years.

CLARE:  Have you seen prices dip before?

HARRY:  This is a collapse, not a dip.

CLARE:  Thirty years is a long time.

HARRY:  Thirty years have tumbled down the hill and piled on top of an old man at the bottom.

CLARE:  Has your address has always been on *(glances at notes)* Monte Verde road?

HARRY:  That's right.

CLARE:  And the name of your farm's Arcadia?

HARRY:  We say Arcadia. *(with Spanish pronunciation, ar-caw-dee-ah with accent on caw)*

CLARE:  How big is it, I mean now?

HARRY:  Sixty-five hectares.

CLARE: I don't know -

HARRY: About a hundred and fifty acres.

CLARE: That's big.

HARRY: Plenty are bigger.

CLARE: Anything else hurting the farmers?

HARRY: Uninvited visitors. And labor. Most pickers are Nica.

CLARE: Nica?

HARRY: From Nicaragua, across the north border. But fewer have been coming since the Sandinistas and Contras stopped killing each other. Now their own coffee production is up and what pickers still come down want to be paid more.

CLARE: Where'd you live in the States?

HARRY: Next to a church.

CLARE: Where -

HARRY: Look, I don't know what you know about farming but this is harvest season and that's when farmers are especially busy.

CLARE: I just have a few more questions. I'm here through Sunday. Could I -

HARRY: I'm really buried right now.

CLARE: Starbucks did say yours was one of the best farms.

HARRY: They said that? . . . Okay here,

*(HARRY gives CLARE his business card.)*

HARRY: it has my cell phone. Sometimes it works. No promises.

CLARE:  All right to walk around?

HARRY:  If you want.

CLARE:  And take pictures?

HARRY:  Shoot away.  You haven't seen anyone else?

CLARE:  Where?

HARRY:  On the farm, or in the offices here or anything?

CLARE:  No, I just got here, remember?

HARRY:  Right.

CLARE:  There was that boy on the bike.

*(CLARE moves to leave.  HARRY stands and she notices his limp.)*

CLARE:  How'd you hurt your leg?

HARRY:  Tractor accident.

CLARE:  Ouch.

HARRY:  Remember how to get out?

CLARE:  I think so.

HARRY:  Don't wander too far off.  One hectare of coffee doesn't look much different from the next.  And it's starting to come down again.

CLARE:  Okay.

HARRY:  You'll see some giant anthills; don't stop to chat.

CLARE:  Okay.

HARRY:  Hasta luego.

*(CLARE doesn't understand.)*

HARRY:  See you later.

CLARE:  Oh, that's right.  Arnold Schwarzenegger.

*(HARRY doesn't get "Terminator" allusion.)*

CLARE:  I told you my Spanish was non-existent.  See you later.  Bye.

*(CLARE exits.  HARRY looks out window, watching CLARE leave.  LOAN enters unseen.  HARRY hears but ignores RIMBAUD.)*

RIMBAUD THE PARROT:  Some things may never happen.  Squawk, squawk.  This one will.

*(A cock crows in the distance, rousing HARRY from his thoughts.  HARRY sees LOAN.)*

HARRY:  Why?  Why?  Why?  Why fucking me?  Who are you?  Where do you come from?  Why have you dropped into my life?  And this infernal silence!  The least you can do is talk while the walls are cracking.
*(succumbs to despair; despair flips to anger)*
Speak goddam you!  Speak!

*(LOAN gives HARRY an aggressive look.  He is afraid.)*

HARRY:  Well if you're not going to leave, at least stay out of my way.  I have a lot to do.

LOAN:  Graves hunger for their tenants.

HARRY:  Unbefuckinglievable.  She can talk.  I don't know what you're saying but at least you can goddam talk.

*(LOAN goes to a plate of half-eaten breakfast.)*

LOAN:  You shouldn't eat meat.

HARRY: What!?

LOAN: That may be an ancestor you had for breakfast.

HARRY: This is what I've been waiting a month to hear, that I'm a cannibal?

LOAN: Do you really want to be eating relatives?

HARRY: I never met them; have you? Maybe they were all assholes. . . Okay, tell me what's in the sausage. If it's anyone I would have cared about I'll throw them up. *(beat)* Are you going to be a permanent fixture now?

LOAN: Nothing's permanent.

HARRY: One of us is crazy and I don't think it's you. If I end up babbling again, these people, all these people on this farm, that's hanging on by a thread this thin . . . What are you doing here?!

LOAN: I meant to get here sooner.

HARRY: What?

LOAN: But I got lost.

HARRY: You got lost?

LOAN: 'fraid so. It was a long way and I'm lousy with directions. I got the coffee farm part right but I came out three hundred kilometers south.

HARRY: What?

LOAN: Scared the bejeezus out of a bunch of Colombians. You should have seen them.

HARRY: Come on, come on, what are you doing here?

LOAN: I'm asking the same thing.

HARRY: And what answer do you get?

LOAN: Our paths, they're connected.

*(In an impulse of curiosity HARRY moves to touch LOAN. LOAN backs away. HARRY moves his hand in front of his eyes to test his vision. LOAN is still there.)*

HARRY: Sometimes you vanish.

LOAN: Yeah, but I don't go far away.

HARRY: Please just show some mercy -

LOAN: Why should I? Did you?

HARRY: What? Please just leave. Vamos por favor. Let's agree this never happened.

LOAN: You know better than that.

HARRY: I want to speak to your superior.

LOAN: Hah, me too. We've never met. You think this is my idea of a good time, hanging out with a depressed bankrupt in Costa Rica?

HARRY: You're pushing it. Depressed maybe, but not bankrupt, not yet anyway. And "hanging out", what shit is that? Not even close. Try torment. You torment, like furies, like devils sneering in some medieval painting. Well go torment someone else.

LOAN: I don't care about anyone else.

HARRY: Why not? Go scare those farmers in Colombia again.

LOAN: There's a harvest to be brought in here.

HARRY: What?

LOAN: It's harvest season, right? Something has to happen.

HARRY: Something is happening. You're driving me fucking crazy!

LOAN:  But I'm not sure what.

HARRY:  For someone from somewhere, from somewhere beyond, there sure is a lot you don't know.  Why do you look  like . . . what you look like . . . like some-one from . . .

LOAN:  From where?

HARRY:  From somewhere on the other side of some world.

LOAN:  Where do you think I come from?

HARRY:  Maybe some mushroom.

LOAN:  I didn't come out of the ground.

HARRY:  That's reassuring; I suppose.  How about from somewhere up here? *(points to his head)*

LOAN:  What a flimsy home that'd be.  In my land you can't see someone like me unless your mind stands on solid ground.

HARRY:  That leaves me out.

LOAN:  That's what I'm thinking too.

HARRY:  My guess is I've made you up.

LOAN:  Why would you have done that?

HARRY:  The alphabet, the letters, you know, the a-b-c's, lately they sometimes fall out the bottom of the words, like how snow falls, and I've been feeling that, that if I don't do something, like something major, like something more than trimming my fingernails, and do it soon, the words, I won't be able to hang on to them and I'll end up ga-ga.

LOAN:  *(taunting)* Like ga-ga, ga-ga-ga-ga.

HARRY: Ohhh shit. I've done ga-ga and well, I'd rather have my leg amputated, this one that's left, without the anaesthetic.

LOAN: So you made me up.

HARRY: Harry's anti-ga-ga fable: "Once upon a time a spirit appeared before Harry." But it ain't working.

LOAN: That's clever.

HARRY: Not clever enough.

LOAN: Around Harry all things revolve. You didn't study Copernicus?

HARRY: You know Copernicus?

LOAN: I saw him at a reception once but he was on the next cloud over.

HARRY: You don't really do that?

LOAN: What?

HARRY: Float around on clouds, like it's happy hour?

LOAN: No, it's never happy hour. That was a joke. Did you create me or not? Once upon a time. Come on, you can tell me.

HARRY: How would I know for sure?

LOAN: Maybe I'm the one who created a fable, about a farmer who thinks he created some spirit creature.

HARRY: Maybe.

LOAN: Here's the deal. I'm stuck, been stuck a long time, stuck in some bottom-less sewer on the other side of death. I've really got to move on.

HARRY: Why are you stuck?

LOAN: Why is the sea blue? All I know is that I can't move on until you move on but I don't know how you'll move on so that we can both move on . . . and I'm expected to do something with you, god knows what.

HARRY: That clears everything up. I don't want to move anywhere.

LOAN: That's not an option.

HARRY: The only good news is that if you're real then it's not all a black hole.

LOAN: If I'm real?

HARRY: Yeah.

LOAN: Oh I'm real Harry. You can bet everything you've got up there.

HARRY: Tell me something I can do, anything, to get you out of here?

LOAN: There is something you cannot do.

HARRY: That's not what I -

LOAN: You're not permitted the easy exit.

HARRY: Oh. . . Maybe I like the taste of cold steel tube, the tickle of hemp on the neck. . . I once tried to turn off the faucet; I don't think it's worth the effort.

LOAN: You just end up in a worse place. Quan Am is my name, vengeance is my game. So take care Harry, take good care.

HARRY: How does our story end?

LOAN: We each have an oar. The shore's not far.

HARRY: That's the best you can do?

LOAN: At least there is not nothing.

HARRY: That's it?

LOAN: As long as we don't whack each other. The absence of nothing should bring a smile. What are you, some kind of idiot?

## ACT 1, SCENE 3

*(That evening, Tuesday. HARRY giving JAVIER Latin lesson.)*

JAVIER: *(reading from a Latin text)* O miserum senem qui mortem contemnendam -

*(HARRY corrects Javier's pronunciation.)*

HARRY: Contemnendam.

JAVIER: Contemnendam.

HARRY: So when was Cicero writing this?

JAVIER: Forty-four BC.

HARRY: What else happened that year?

JAVIER: They killed Caesar?

HARRY: Yes, he had a rough day at the Forum didn't he? And so did Rome. Cicero saw it all sliding down the drain. In less than a year the war will have his head too, literally. Translate that bit.

*(JAVIER picks up his handwritten study notes.)*

HARRY: No, no, work on your sight reading.

JAVIER: "O wretched man who does not see that death
*(stumbling)*

HARRY:  Must not be feared.

JAVIER:  "Must not be feared.  Which" -

HARRY:  What's the antecedent?

JAVIER:  Death?

HARRY:  No, fear of death.  There's a difference.

*(LOAN enters and observes.  HARRY does not see her.)*

HARRY:  Precision, Javi, precision.

JAVIER:  Right.

HARRY:  Thought requires language and language requires precision.  The alternative is mobs, madmen and gibberish.

JAVIER:  *(showing off)* Precision, from praecido, praecidere, praecedi, praecisum, third conjugation transitive, to cut off.

HARRY:  I said precision, not exhibition.  And the perfect is praecidi, not praecedi.  Language wants precision the way a woman wants love.

JAVIER:  How does a woman want love?

HARRY:  I'm flunking that class right now.  Cicero's an old man here, aware of his own mortality and depressed about his beloved Rome.

JAVIER:  You're not like really old but you seem so tired lately, and worried, like all the time.

HARRY:  You worry about your studies.

JAVIER:  Is that American bothering you?

HARRY:  There've been way too many visitors lately.  How'd practice go?

JAVIER:  I had trouble getting into it.  Coach chewed my butt out.

HARRY:  Practice or a game, never let up.

JAVIER:  Hey, but the shoe stayed on.

HARRY:  Good old duct tape.  Have you filled out your college applications?

JAVIER:  The ones for Spain are done.

HARRY:  Be sure you apply here too.  Now I don't know if I'll have the money for Europe or America.

JAVIER:  I kinda figured.  I can get them all finished next week.  We're out for Christmas break.

HARRY:  And I'm going to need your help.  All the prunings need to be piled together and burned.  Maybe the rain'll stop.

JAVIER:  Si Padre.

HARRY:  No Javi, my name is Harry, Harry Howell the farmer.  We've talked about -

JAVIER:  But -

HARRY:  Your padre was killed in a war.

JAVIER:  But I don't even remember him.

HARRY:  Well I do; I buried him.  Come on, who needs a father anyway?  Does Rimbaud give a hoot who his father was?

RIMBAUD THE PARROT:  Squawk.

JAVIER:  If you don't like Padre shouldn't I get to pick some other name for you?

HARRY:  Like what?

JAVIER: *(beat)* I don't know . . . Grumpy, from the seven dwarves.

HARRY: Harry works just fine.

*(JAVIER is downcast, gathers his books and starts to leave.)*

HARRY: Remember: "Always be the best my boy, the bravest, and hold your head high -

JAVIER: *(perks up)* above the others." The Iliad.

HARRY: Always be the best my boy,

JAVIER: *(perky)* The bravest.

*(JAVIER exits. When LOAN speaks HARRY becomes aware of her presence.)*

LOAN: If anyone knows what it means to need a father, it should be you.

HARRY: Oh, is that right? And just what else do you know?

LOAN: How Father Finnegan would wake you boys up in the orphanage. *(mimics Father Finnegan)* "Morning lads! Let go of your cocks and put on your socks. Up and at 'em." How cold that wooden floor was on winter mornings.

HARRY: How do you -

*(LOAN gestures "There's a lot that I know." After initial shock HARRY allows himself to briefly enjoy the memory.)*

HARRY: The smell of licorice, that always brings him back; the Father loved Black Jack gum. Boy, did he have a nasty temper, if you were dumb enough to cross him. *(breaks reverie)* Leave me alone! Calling me Padre disrespects his real father.

LOAN: Look at it from Javi's eyes. He never knew that Nica. In ninety-nine out of a hundred ways you are his father. Don't fight that.

HARRY: Don't tell me what to do! This is language. It deserves precision.

LOAN: No, this is a boy. He deserves a father.

*(JAVIER enters unseen to retrieve something. Halts at doorway and watches HARRY talking seemingly to the air.)*

HARRY: Forget it.

LOAN: No -

HARRY: You don't know shit about how a boy becomes a man.

*(JAVIER exits unseen by HARRY.)*

## ACT 1, SCENE 4

*(Morning next day, Wednesday. HARRY and CARLOS in meeting.)*

HARRY: Are you wearing smaller pants these days?

CARLOS: It's Teresa's cooking. You think I should go shopping?

HARRY: Wouldn't hurt. Do you think the price has hit bottom yet?

CARLOS: Maybe for pants.

RIMBAUD THE PARROT: Hope is the thing with feathers. Squawk.

CARLOS: *(startled, then laughs)* When you'd get that?

RIMBAUD THE PARROT: That lurches in the soul.

HARRY: *(to RIMBAUD)* Perches, it's perches, perches in the soul! *(to CARLOS)* A few years back.

RIMBAUD THE PARROT: Perches in the -

HARRY: *(to RIMBAUD)* That's enough!

RIMBAUD THE PARROT: Squawk.

CARLOS: He's a noisy bastard. If the price goes much lower we'll be giving the beans away. How are Dora and Javier?

HARRY: Fine. Javi's going to university next year.

CARLOS: Zshee, when I left he was just starting school.

HARRY: Zshee is right. He's done well. Hey, last year after a co-op meeting you asked that I talk to you, talk to you first if I ever thought about selling.

CARLOS: Yes.

HARRY: Well I'm thinking of shrinking the farm, making it a bit more manageable.

CARLOS: How much shrinking?

HARRY: Maybe carving off the land south of the stream.

CARLOS: Wow, wasn't expecting this. Look who's asking for whose help now.

HARRY: It's an opportunity, not help.

CARLOS: Why should I do any favors for you?

HARRY: What do you mean?

CARLOS: For someone who fired me.

HARRY: No one is asking for a favor and that was centuries ago. The only reason to buy my land is because it's a good deal for you.

CARLOS: And that would depend on the price.

HARRY: That's right. You know this place better than anyone else.

CARLOS: How much land do you have south of the stream?

HARRY: Forty hectares.

CARLOS:  You know I didn't do it.

HARRY:  Didn't do what?

CARLOS:  You know what. I didn't take that money.

HARRY:  Doesn't matter now. That was what, fifteen years ago?

CARLOS:  Thirteen.

HARRY:  Ancient history.

CARLOS:  You never had proof.

HARRY:  Let's leave the past alone.

CARLOS:  Can't do that.

HARRY:  You never understood how lucky you were to only lose your job.

CARLOS:  It hurt my reputation.

HARRY:  Come on, now you own one of the biggest farms in the valley. In fact I'm hurt that you never thanked me. If you had stayed on here you wouldn't have ended up rich.

CARLOS:  Not working for El Gringo Monopata, the tightest farmer in the valley.

HARRY:  Now who's hurting whose reputation? Look, if you're not interested there are lots of farmers who will be. I'm trying to be nice here, talking to you first.

CARLOS:  I'll need a couple of days.

HARRY:  If you're interested you need to let me know by this weekend.

CARLOS:  We'll see.

HARRY:  Thanks for coming by.

## ACT 1, SCENE 5

*(Evening two days later, Friday. HARRY is concluding a Latin tutorial with JAVIER. A crutch can be seen nearby. After scene begins CLARE enters and stands in doorway, unseen by HARRY and JAVIER.)*

HARRY: No, "vivo Caesare" is ablative absolute: "when Caesar was alive." Why do I bother if you're not going to make the effort?

JAVIER: I am making an effort.

HARRY: You might at least make an effort to disguise your lack of effort.

JAVIER: But I am working at it. I am working hard. It's not easy, you know. Plus school's not out yet and I am helping with the harvest and I'm still playing futbol and lately . . .

HARRY: Yes?

JAVIER: Nothing.

HARRY: Nothing my rear-end. Come on.

JAVIER: Lately, your words . . .

HARRY: Yes, I have lots of words.

JAVIER: Don't I know. You've always been so good with them but now sometimes . . . you come up empty.

HARRY: I have a lot on my mind.

JAVIER: Maybe it's gottten too crowded up there.

HARRY: Must be it. The words are having traffic jams.

JAVIER: I'm worried something's wrong.

HARRY: Something is wrong; the coffee price is the lowest in twenty years.

JAVIER: No . . . aw forget it.

HARRY: No, you spit it out.

JAVIER: The stoics, those guys, well next to you lately they have the giggles.

HARRY: The stoics? That's good Javi, at least it hasn't been a total waste. Let me tell you what to worry about - your studies and pulling your weight around here. Do you hear me?

JAVIER: I -

*(HARRY and JAVIER notice CLARE.)*

JAVIER: Hi.

CLARE: Hello.

HARRY: *(to JAVIER)* Keep working on Cicero, chapter thirty-five. Try harder, don't let him beat you.

*(JAVIER exits.)*

CLARE: Will I get an assignment?

HARRY: You already do: get your degree and move to Seattle.

CLARE: You know Greek?

HARRY: A little. That was Latin.

CLARE: Is there much difference?

HARRY: The Adriatic Sea and an alphabet. To start with.

CLARE: Are you always the demanding professor?

HARRY: Only when my leg's off. Hand it to me.

CLARE:  Hand you what?

HARRY:  A leg.  My leg. *(points)* Over there.

*(CLARE, taken aback because she's never touched a prosthesis, hands it to him.)*

CLARE:  A tractor did that?

*(HARRY points to a spot halfway up leg.)*

HARRY:  If this was Italy, here would be Rome.

*(HARRY points to a piece of fabric that had been near the prothesis.)*

HARRY:  That too.

*(Using two fingers like it's a dirty diaper, CLARE picks up fabric.)*

HARRY:  It won't hurt you.

CLARE:  What is it?

HARRY:  A stump sock.  It goes on my stump.

CLARE:  On your -

*(CLARE points to his knee.)*

HARRY:  That's right.

CLARE:  Why do you do that?

HARRY:  So I can walk.  You know, be a normal bipedal primate.

CLARE:  No, the professor bit.

HARRY:  It helps with the monotony.

CLARE:  Come on, it's gorgeous here.

HARRY: Right now the sun sets at five-thirty.  Know when it sets in the summer?

*(CLARE nods "no".)*

HARRY: Six.  Tropical ennui.  We do what we can to fight it.

CLARE: Are you like his tutor?

HARRY: No.

CLARE: But he's like your student?

HARRY: No, like my orphan.  He's adopted.

CLARE: And Dora?

HARRY: Like his mother.  Look -

CLARE: I know you're really busy.

HARRY: The professor.

CLARE: No, you know, harvest season, I made a note.  You said the biggest problem is low price.  What's behind that?

*(HARRY pours himself a stiff drink.)*

HARRY: Want a drink?

CLARE: No thank you.

HARRY: Sure?

CLARE: I'm sure.

HARRY: Why not?

CLARE: I don't drink.

HARRY: You have a drinking problem?

CLARE: No. Do you?

HARRY: I have lots of problems.

CLARE: Lots of us do.

HARRY: It helps with the balance.

CLARE: So, the coffee price problem?

*(HARRY goes to the globe and turns it.)*

HARRY: There're lots of factors but the biggest is that the World Bank in its infinite wisdom has been funding new coffee farms in Vietnam. And those farms are now dumping production on the world supply and even though they're growing low quality Robusta beans, it's still dragging down prices everywhere including for the Arabica beans we grow here. Vietnam's destroying Arcadia.

CLARE: Does anyone here grow Robusta?

HARRY: Robusta is crap that we don't touch in Costa Rica.

CLARE: How do you get all this international information?

HARRY: Trade magazines tell me what I need to know.

CLARE: Was it hard to set up down here, buy a farm and all that?

HARRY: What does that have to do with coffee prices?

CLARE: I know you didn't see my letter but my professor wants me to include a profile of an actual farmer. You know, anchor my research in a real farm. The people at the co-op suggested you.

*(HARRY doesn't want to cooperate but remembers Clare's claim that Starbucks executives will read her thesis.)*

HARRY: Looked for your letter this morning, couldn't find anything.

CLARE: They say you know more about coffee than anyone in the valley.

HARRY: Don't know why they would say that.

CLARE: And they say you know everyone, that you were even president of the co-op.

HARRY: Ten years ago.

CLARE: And that you know people in government too.

HARRY: Hardly a recommendation. Leave my farm out of it.

CLARE: I can let you read it before I turn it in.

HARRY: No.

CLARE: Why not?

HARRY: Most people go through life trying to get the world to notice them. My goal's been the opposite.

CLARE: How come?

HARRY: A keen appreciation of our insignificance.

CLARE: That sounds like something a philosopher or poet would say.

HARRY: I'm a farmer who grows an Ethiopian shrub in order to extract the pit inside its fruit and then sell it. Inconsequential? Completely. But nothing compared to poets. They hold the world record for insignificance.

CLARE: Do farmers even think about poets?

HARRY: In Rome they did. Read Virgil.

*(CLARE pulls out piece of paper.)*

CLARE: I did some research and stumbled on something: "Caw-cawing, the crow punctures blue sky / Draws down a shade blacker than his eye. / Sight is silenced. No time left to die."

HARRY: Yeah?

CLARE: Ring any bell?

HARRY: *(with menace)* Could wring a neck.

CLARE: *(a little afraid)* What do you mean?

HARRY: Nothing, darling, means nothing to me. "No time left to die"? Doesn't even make sense.

CLARE: I did more research, about the poet who wrote that.

HARRY: Necks are fragile. You're wasting my time.

CLARE: It's brief. *(retrieves notes)* In nineteen sixty-eight there was a young poet named Harrison Shaw who had a book published. That year he dropped out of Fordham, joined the Navy, trained as a medical corpsman, had a leg shredded by shrapnel in Vietnam, got the Purple Heart.

HARRY: This poet, when he came home did they go *(makes spitting action)* on him?

CLARE: Don't know, but run over, almost anyway.

HARRY: Run over?

CLARE: Had a traffic accident - hit by a car. And then disappeared. His driver's license - New York, expired - washed up from the East River a few days later. Presumed suicide.

HARRY: One more war casualty.

CLARE: They never found a body.

*(As RIMBAUD speaks, LOAN enters unseen.)*

RIMBAUD THE PARROT: If any question why we died.

HARRY: Just ignore him.

RIMBAUD THE PARROT: Tell them because -

HARRY: *(to RIMBAUD)* That's enough Rimbaud.

*(HARRY gets himself another drink. Pours a small amount into a receptacle in Rimbaud's cage.)*

RIMBAUD THE PARROT: Our fathers lied.

HARRY: *(to RIMBAUD)* Drink up.

RIMBAUD THE PARROT: Cheers.

HARRY: *(to CLARE; off her surprise)* He fell off the perch a long time ago. An overactive imagination can get you in trouble.

CLARE: Trouble?

HARRY: Big deep-shit trouble.

CLARE: How?

HARRY: These latitudes, they can be treacherous.

CLARE: That sounds like a warning.

HARRY: Fact. Life is cheap at the tenth parallel.

CLARE: You said the tropics were boring.

HARRY: Also dangerous. You heard me.

CLARE:  You never really answered my question.  Why are you teaching a boy Latin on a coffee farm?

HARRY:  Where else would I be teaching him?

CLARE:  I just -

HARRY:  *(with anger)* What, the poor Latino orphan doesn't deserve to learn the language that bore his language?  Or maybe it's too tough for him?

CLARE:  Whoa, hold on.  I was just asking - Are you always like this?

HARRY:  Like what this?

CLARE:  So charming, this -

HARRY:  I'm famous for it.

*(HARRY becomes aware of LOAN; falters.  CLARE is confused.)*

CLARE:  So why the Latin?

HARRY:  The boy enjoys it.

CLARE:  Didn't look -

HARRY:  Some of the time he does.  The nights will come when despair will bludgeon him into quivering pulp.  Ka-bup, ka-bup, ka-bup - *(sound of a rapid heartbeat)* ever had one of those?

CLARE:  As a matter of fact -

HARRY:  Authors, the really good ones, they can reach a hand across centuries and pull you back from the abyss.

*(HARRY refills his glass.)*

HARRY:  But only - and it's a big "but only" - if you've earned their regard through study.  Otherwise they don't give a shit about you.

CLARE: Sounds like some religion.

HARRY: No, like friendship. You take their book and instead of you holding it, the author holds you. They offer you the illusion that you're not alone.

CLARE: Have they done that for you?

HARRY: On occasion. Up 'til now.

*(HARRY's aggression is spent. He looks at his watch.)*

CLARE: It's late.

HARRY: Yes.

CLARE: I have to drive back to Grecia.

HARRY: *(looks at the sky)* No moon out tonight. The roads are wet and ink-black.

CLARE: I'll drive slow. I can find my way.

HARRY: If you have an accident the police are going to be back here waking me up. . . . If you want, Dora can make up a place for you to sleep.

CLARE: No thanks.

HARRY: Have you ever driven roads this black?

CLARE: That'd be too much trouble.

HARRY: Trouble is police knocking on my door at midnight.

CLARE: Are you sure it's okay?

HARRY: Ask Dora if you don't believe me.

CLARE: *(takes a moment)* Okay, but only if you promise it's no bother.

HARRY: What did I say? . . . Stay focused on the coffee.

CLARE:  What?

HARRY:  Your research.  I'll find Dora.  Good night.  *(starts to exit)*

CLARE:  Good night.


## ACT 1, SCENE 6

*(Middle of Friday night.  No dialog.  CLARE sleeps on couch.  LOAN enters.  She is imagining what it would be like to be mortal and fertile.  She pulls back CLARE's blanket, ponders her, cups a breast and lightly squeezes, places a hand over CLARE's womb. CLARE cannot perceive LOAN's touch.  LOAN pulls the blanket back up and exits.)*


## ACT 1, SCENE 7

*(Early morning, next day, Saturday.  DORA at the desk working with accounting papers and a 10-key adding machine set on non-print mode.  CLARE, lying on couch where she has recently wakened, watches DORA.  CLARE sits up.)*

DORA:  Good morning.

CLARE:  Hi.

*(DORA continues working.  CLARE looks around.)*

DORA:  There's coffee there.

CLARE:  *(taking a sip)* Umm, super.  Where did this come from?

DORA:  Well, from right out there.

CLARE:  *(pause)* I mean this morning. . . . Thank you.

DORA:  Don't thank me.

CLARE: Why not?

DORA: Not necessary. I was making it anyway.

CLARE: That was nice.

DORA: If we only get one thing right around here it should be a cup of coffee.

CLARE: Well, it is delicious, and that was really nice.

DORA: You said that.

CLARE: Thanks for letting me barge in, then putting me up last night. . . Where's Harry?

DORA: Why?

CLARE: I don't know.

DORA: Out with the pickers. He has meetings back here later.

CLARE: This morning I'm going to visit the co-op factory, the beni-, how do you say that?

DORA: Beneficio.

CLARE: Beneficio. Then I was hoping to interview Harry one last time. I fly back tomorrow.

DORA: You two sure were talking for a long time last night.

CLARE: I have to get more background. Part of my thesis will be about this farm in particular. . . . Harry doesn't like talking much about his past.

DORA: Some men have no past.

CLARE: That's not true, everyone has a past.

*(CLARE starts to fold bedding and continues that business while talking.)*

DORA:  You don't need to do that.

CLARE:  It's nothing.

DORA:  You must have had a lot of questions.

CLARE:  More questions than he had answers.

DORA:  He got up around midnight and never came back.

CLARE:  We weren't talking that late.

DORA:  What were you doing?

CLARE:  Trying to get answers.

DORA:  That's all?

CLARE:  I'm just trying to understand . . . to finish this thesis so I can get on with my life.

DORA:  I see.  Just be sure not to drink from someone else's cup.

CLARE:  Look, you don't think, you can't -

DORA:  Why can't I?

CLARE:  You're joking, right?  Harry could be, I mean he's old enough to be my father.

DORA:  So?

CLARE:  No way.  Ugghh.

DORA:  Why ugghh?

CLARE:  Oh, for just about a thousand reasons.

DORA:  Is he looking that bad?

CLARE:  No, that's not one of them.

DORA:  Sometimes when men lose their balance they grab on to the nearest thing.

CLARE:  No worries. As soon as you gave me these *(the bedding)* I was out to the world.  Has he always hit the booze so hard?

DORA:  He's under huge pressure.

CLARE:  That doesn't really help.

DORA:  He's spent his whole life building this farm and now it's falling apart in front of him.  What would you know about that?

CLARE:  A little about things falling apart and a lot about the booze.  It'll kill him if he doesn't watch it.  I'd say the parrot is at risk too.

RIMBAUD THE PARROT:  Squawk.

DORA:  *(to RIMBAUD)* Buenos dias.

RIMBAUD THE PARROT:  Squawk.

DORA:  Shhh. *(to CLARE)* What would you know about falling apart?

CLARE:  I buried someone last month.  After a life wallowing in that stuff.

DORA:  Who?

CLARE:  And it wasn't pretty.  In fact I don't think it gets much uglier.  My father.

DORA:  I'm sorry.

CLARE:  Could I ask you a couple of questions?

DORA:  For your - ?

CLARE:  Yeah.  Just one or two.

*(CLARE gets out notebook and pen.)*

CLARE:  When did you start working here?

DORA:  Ten years ago.

CLARE:  How long have you been married?

*(DORA, embarrassed, does not reply.)*

CLARE:  Ooh, I'm sorry.  Stepped in it there, didn't I?  I just assumed -

DORA:  Don't assume.

CLARE:  No.  You obviously are Harry's right hand.

DORA:  I keep the books balanced.

CLARE:  What did Harry do before, in the U.S.?

DORA:  He's the man with no past, remember?

CLARE:  Has he ever mentioned any woman from back then?

DORA:  What kind of woman?

CLARE:  A painter.

DORA:  Never mentioned any painter.

CLARE:  Nothing at all?

DORA:  Sorry.

RIMBAUD THE PARROT:  Some things may never happen.

DORA:  *(to RIMBAUD)* Yes, we see you.

RIMBAUD THE PARROT: This one will. Squawk.

DORA: Our painted chicken doesn't like to be ignored.

CLARE: He doesn't look like he's in too good of shape right now.

DORA: Rimbaud's healthy as a horse.

CLARE: Harry.

DORA: Like I said, he's under huge pressure.

CLARE: How bad is it, for Arcadia?

DORA: *(lifts papers)* That's what I'm trying to figure out. Every farmer's in trouble. . . I don't think this should be in your -

CLARE: No, it won't be.

DORA: Harry could lose everything.

CLARE: Would that mean you'd lose everything too?

DORA: Not like Harry.

CLARE: Where would you go?

DORA: I'm not sure. I have a sister and mother in San Jose. Maybe I could stay with them a while.

CLARE: And Javier? Harry was laying into him last night.

DORA: What do you mean?

CLARE: With that Greek or Latin or whatever. I wouldn't want to be in his classroom.

DORA: Don't judge too fast.

CLARE: Am I?

DORA: Yes. That boy means the world and then some to Harry. He says those books will help Javi grow up to be a good man.

CLARE: Well if that's love or whatever, I don't see it.

DORA: Javi doesn't always see it either.

CLARE: He's an impressive boy. And lucky I guess to have been adopted.

DORA: They were both lucky.

CLARE: Maybe their best luck was the day you walked in here.

DORA: I just pay the bills and take care of the guys. Where's yours?

CLARE: Nowhere. *(spins globe)* Nowhere on here at all. Who'd want to get involved with a mess like me?

DORA: Soon to graduate with a job at Starbucks headquarters? Doesn't sound too bad.

CLARE: Sounds better than it is. It can't be easy loving a man like Harry, the man with no past and all.

DORA: It's not much to love someone who's easy to love.

CLARE: No.

DORA: The trick is to make sure they're worth loving in the first place.

CLARE: How can you tell?

DORA: Some say prayer.

CLARE: Is that what you say?

DORA: I say we're corks bobbing on the ocean and sometimes the right ones bump into each other. And when the waves get rough you both hang on.

## ACT 1, SCENE 8

*(Later that morning, Saturday. HARRY and CARLOS  negotiating.)*

CARLOS:  What price do you have in mind?

HARRY:  Last year Romero got nine million colones per hectare and my land is better.

CARLOS:  And since then the coffee price has fallen what, another twelve, fifteen percent?  No way Romero would get that today. . . Is Starbucks still buying your beans?

HARRY:  About half of them.  They pay good but it still doesn't come close to covering our costs.

CARLOS:  Prices will come back eventually.  When you were co-op president this valley was swimming in money.  Remember those dancers in the swimming pool at the Christmas party?

*(HARRY just looks at him.)*

CARLOS:  Are the cabins still there?

HARRY:  They better be since I've got pickers staying in them.  We painted them last summer - sky blue.  Including the one where we found them.

CARLOS:  So they'd be part of the deal.

HARRY:  Well I'm not about to move them.

*(HARRY picks up stray paper, looks at it, crumples it into a ball and keeps fidgeting with it.)*

CARLOS:  Finding Javi's family was a nasty business.

HARRY:  You weren't much help as I recall.

CARLOS: I was at my brother's in Alajuela. We had gotten drunk and I didn't want to drive back. But I was here the next morning and Javi screaming over his dead mother didn't do anything for my hangover.

HARRY: The police never came up with anything.

CARLOS: They say he had been involved with the Contras in Managua and the Sandinistas tracked him down here. Does Javi remember anything?

HARRY: No, we guess he was three.

CARLOS: He's lucky there. It's not every night a kid sees his parents get shot.

HARRY: No.

CARLOS: That was a long time ago.

HARRY: War.

*(LOAN enters. HARRY sees her and is distressed.)*

CARLOS: Yeah war. Over now.

HARRY: Not so easy to forget.

CARLOS: Why not? Wasn't our war. The goddam Nicas should have kept it on their side of the border. . . You all right?

HARRY: *(recovers somewhat)* War's a nasty business.

CARLOS: What do you know about it?

HARRY: I was a soldier once.

CARLOS: Sure you were.

HARRY: A long ago soldier in a far away war.

CARLOS: Right. And what war would that have been?

HARRY: The Punic Wars. That's when this happened.

*(HARRY points to his leg.)*

CARLOS: What?

HARRY: An elephant stepped on it. Hannibal surprised us with those elephants.

CARLOS: You're losing it Harry.

*(HARRY lobs the paper wad in Carlos's general direction; makes soft missile-flying sound and, when it hits floor, an explosion sound. HARRY and LOAN make eye contact.)*

HARRY: I know.

CARLOS: I say sell everything. Cash in all your chips and move back.

HARRY: To the States?

CARLOS: Yeah.

HARRY: Nothing back there but bad memories and lying politicians.

CARLOS: *(laughing)* They lie here too.

HARRY: Yeah but with no army they do less damage. Sorry, I'm not moving anywhere. This is my home.

CARLOS: You'd have a fat cushion to pay for university and buy you and Dora a nice place.

HARRY: Costa Rica is my home.

CARLOS: But -

HARRY: Let me try to help you here. Do you know Nuestra Madre cemetery?

CARLOS: Sure, that's where my mother is buried.

HARRY:  Then she'll be my neighbor because that's where my grave is.

CARLOS:  My mother may not like that.

HARRY:  We don't always get what we want, do we?  How did she die?

CARLOS:  Without seeing her son.

HARRY:  How -

CARLOS:  She died when I was born.

HARRY:  Well, I'll be keeping her company.  All I did coming here was continue America's great tradition.

CARLOS:  What tradition?

HARRY:  Pulling up stakes, heading west, reinventing ourselves.

CARLOS:  But you came south.

HARRY:  I was having problems with my compass.

CARLOS:  Maybe your compass will work this time.

HARRY:  Old coffee plants don't survive transplanting.  You know that.

CARLOS:  I don't think too old to head north, with a fat bank balance and one good leg.

HARRY:  Do you believe in ghosts?

CARLOS:  Okay, see what I mean about losing it?  Cash is going to be a problem for any buyer.

HARRY:  Less so with your father-in-law.

CARLOS:  Turns out he's not going to be much help.

HARRY: His bank's still making plenty of money.

CARLOS: I bumped into him at a hotel in San Jose last week.

HARRY: Yeah, what hotel?

CARLOS: The hotel wasn't the problem. Who was with me was. She was a she and she wasn't Teresa. Now I've got problems at home and the bank.

HARRY: A hotel in San Jose? Not too smart Carlos.

CARLOS: Hey, I was pressed for time.

HARRY: Has some cute American business student visited you this week?

CARLOS: No, but you can always send cute my way.

HARRY: She interviewed me and said she was going to visit your farm.

CARLOS: Haven't seen her. You'll be lucky to get six million per hectare.

HARRY: Six million would be robbery.

CARLOS: It seems that you have two options: sell or let the bank foreclose and they sell. And don't accuse me of robbery a second time.

*(CARLOS starts to leave.)*

CARLOS: If your price doesn't come down then I'm not your buyer. Try Romero; since he sold his land for so much he can afford to buy yours.

HARRY: Romero's smarter than us; he got out of farming.

CARLOS: Can I make a suggestion?

*(CARLOS retrieves paper wad and tosses it in the waste basket.)*

CARLOS: When you talk about selling your land don't bring up elephants and war shit.

HARRY: You're the one who asked about the cabins.

RIMBAUD THE PARROT: Let us go then -

CARLOS: I'm trying to be helpful Harry, despite -

RIMBAUD THE PARROT: You and I.

HARRY: You should be more careful about your hotels, and your women.

CARLOS: Oh there was nothing wrong with her, trust me.

HARRY: And you shouldn't drink so much.

CARLOS: Forgive me father for I have sinned. They say you're drunk every night now.

HARRY: They lie.

CARLOS: That's what they're saying in town. Know what else? They're making bets on what's going to collapse first - you or your farm.

HARRY: The answer's neither.

CARLOS: If you decide to come down to the real world, you have my number.

HARRY: I need to look at budgets with Dora.

(*CARLOS exits.*)

LOAN: I liked the elephants. That was good.

HARRY: You liked the elephants. Just fucking great.

## ACT 1, SCENE 9

*(That afternoon, Saturday. HARRY and DORA are reviewing budgets. HARRY drinking a beer.)*

HARRY:  Would we really need the second truck then?

DORA:  No, you could sell the Toyota.

HARRY:  What else can we cut?

*(A knock at the partially open door. JAVIER enters with CLARE behind him and points backward under his arm toward CLARE.)*

JAVIER:  Your visitor is here again.

CLARE:  Sorry to be interrupting.  I can wait out here while, you know, you finish your meeting.  I thought I'd be here hours ago.

*(JAVIER turns to leave.)*

HARRY:  *(to JAVIER)* Nice shoes.

*(JAVIER displays a bit of fancy soccer footwork in his new shoes as he exits.)*

CLARE:  Am I too late?

HARRY:  Do you get to your classes at Columbia on time?

CLARE:  I didn't expect to spend so much time at the beneficio.  Cesar was really a big help.

HARRY:  You caught him on a good day.

CLARE:  At least a busy day.  That place is cranking right now.

HARRY:  Yeah, well, it is harvest season.

DORA:  *(to HARRY)* Those are rough numbers.  I'm still not sure about this.

*(Desk phone rings. HARRY answers it.)*

HARRY: Bueno. . . Thanks for calling back. . . . What?! I just need the brakes fixed, not a new engine! It's a twenty year old tractor for god's sake. . . . If your prices were as good as your bullshit . . . That's ridiculous. I'll get someone else to fix the brakes!

*(HARRY hangs up the phone.)*

DORA: So there's a budget to look at anyway. *(to CLARE)* We just finished. Good to see you.

CLARE: Thanks. Good to see you too.

DORA: Don't let him bite your head off.

*(DORA exits.)*

CLARE: I thought I'd just have a few more questions but of course now I have a hundred. And I know I'll have more when I get back to New York. Is it okay to call you then, on your phone, now that it seems to be working?

HARRY: If it's still working.

CLARE: Thanks. *(gets out notebook and pen)* So, can you tell me about production per plant?

HARRY: You really want to know this stuff?

CLARE: Well yes, I want to turn in a good thesis and graduate.

HARRY: Right; and work at Starbucks headquarters.

CLARE: That's right.

HARRY: A plant by its third year produces twelve kilos of cherries. That's on a good farm.

CLARE: Per year?

HARRY: Yes, one plant, per year, good farm, twelve kilos. It keeps that up until its twentieth year.

CLARE: Then what?

HARRY: After twenty years it gets ripped out and replaced.

CLARE: And how high up is your farm, its elevation?

HARRY: Perfect for Arabica. . . . Look, I can talk about coffee 'til the goats quit eating but let's stop playing games. I want to know who you are and what you want.

CLARE: I don't know what you mean.

HARRY: Yes you do. That MBA stuff is crap. I don't think you're really who you say you are.

CLARE: You're accusing someone of not being who they say they are?

HARRY: Precisely. You've done an impressive job of acting.

CLARE: Call the B-School at Columbia if you don't believe me.

HARRY: I did.

CLARE: Okay. So?

HARRY: They never heard of Clare Gutterman.

CLARE: Maybe you talked to the wrong person.

HARRY: Starbucks never heard of you either.

CLARE: Well I don't work there yet, do I?

HARRY: Nor has Carlos Alvarado.

CLARE: I haven't got to his farm yet.

HARRY:  You're full of crap.

CLARE:  You're full of booze.

HARRY:  That's enough!  It's time young lady

*(HARRY picks up beer bottle and moves toward CLARE.  CLARE backs up.)*

HARRY:  for you - Afraid?  What of?

CLARE:  I'm not afraid of -

HARRY:  What does some poet who drowned have to do with you?

CLARE:  After Walter Reed Hospital he returned to New York where he ran out into traffic on Riverside Drive and was committed to the psych ward at Bellevue. There he met an artist named Virginia Easton.  A week later Easton jumped from Bellevue's roof.

HARRY:  You sure you got all that straight?  Why are you trying to dig up the dead, some poet no one heard of and some painter no one heard of?

CLARE:  Someone did.

HARRY:  Who?

CLARE:  Me.

HARRY:  How?

CLARE:  She's my mother.

*(HARRY takes a moment.  Sees that his beer is empty and pours himself a stiff drink.)*

HARRY:  Go home to Daddy.

CLARE:  I can't.

HARRY:  Why not?

CLARE:  There's not one.

HARRY:  Home or Daddy?

CLARE:  When she died, however she died, she left behind a baby.

HARRY:  Join the club.  And get out.

(INTERMISSION)

# *ACT 2*

## SCENE 1

*(Continuation of previous scene. Clare still afraid but stands her ground. Pulls papers and a small book from her bag.)*

CLARE:  You want me to get out?  Like Harrison Shaw got out thirty years ago.

HARRY:  You said drowned.  The East River coughed up his wallet.

CLARE:  But not his body.

HARRY:  What is that?

CLARE:  Poetry.

HARRY:  Where'd you get it?

CLARE:  Paul had a storage locker in the Meat district.

HARRY:  Who's Paul?

CLARE:  The Daddy you told me to go home to.  Who died last month.  I found all kinds of things in his locker.

HARRY:  If you had half a brain that's where you would have left them.

CLARE:  *(reading from book jacket)* "Mr. Shaw's debut has exploded on the literary landscape with more devastating power than our bombs now pounding Vietnam."

HARRY:  Written with a toilet brush.

CLARE:  The review or the poetry?

HARRY: Don't know the poetry.

CLARE: Maybe your memory needs a toilet brush.

HARRY: What you need -

CLARE: Were you ever a poet?

HARRY: Ha! You think I could have been one of those? Horace and Homer and Housman and this Harrison Shaw? One of those alliterative assholes?

CLARE: What's alliterative?

HARRY: I'll fuck forty firemen before I tell you. Do I look like a poet?

CLARE: I wouldn't know.

HARRY: Actually I did know some poets. The Village was crawling with them. Anyone who walked into a coffee shop with Kafka in his pocket could call himself a poet. But none of them looked anything like this sack of bones.

CLARE: I read his poetry.

HARRY: So?

CLARE: There's a lot of, I don't know, pain and stuff in it.

HARRY: Pain? Right. The only thing that pains me is visitors and coffee prices. Poets think they examine the heart and illuminate the truth. Poets don't illuminate shit. The only things I examine are leaves for signs of fungus and financials for red ink. You got that?

CLARE: Yeah, okay.

HARRY: I grow coffee. In a good year I sell it for more than I spend to grow it. It's that simple. What you have down here is real life: people trying to keep a roof over their head, food on their table, the flapping wings far away. Fuck your poets, they're ink shitters.

RIMBAUD THE PARROT:  Now smacks a noble heart.

HARRY:  Cracks!  Cracks a fucking noble heart.

RIMBAUD THE PARROT:  Good night, sweet Prince.

HARRY:  Still afternoon; shut up.

CLARE:  Who taught him that stuff?

HARRY:  He came that way.

CLARE:  You sure have strong opinions about poets.

HARRY:  I'm an opinionated sort of guy.  What, you haven't noticed?  If this poet didn't take his final bath in the East River, then what did happen to him?

*(CLARE holds up an old envelope.)*

CLARE:  Shaw wrote my dad a letter a year after my mother jumped, asking where she was buried.  Postmark is Costa Rica.  Where were you in nineteen sixty-nine?

HARRY:  Out of country.

CLARE:  Where out of country?

HARRY:  Overseas.

*(CLARE retrieves from her bag a note written in crayon and a small wrapped object which she keeps in her hand.  Reads.)*

CLARE:  "When they brought me here I was shrivelled, shattered and bruised. You are my healer.  Your bravery puts me to shame.  In deepest gratitude I give you my heart."

HARRY:  Shrivelled, shattered, bruised.  And this guy was a poet?  Well shiver me shattered teak timbers.  Adolescent  excrement.

CLARE:  You knew Shaw wrote that.

HARRY: Why else would you have it?

CLARE: I don't think Shaw is writing a poem here.

HARRY: I don't either.

CLARE: No. He's trying to save himself and is thanking someone for throwing him a rope. They were both trying to save themselves and each other.

HARRY: I told you to leave. Get out.

CLARE: Why?

HARRY: Because you're obsessed and a liar and I have much bigger problems.

CLARE: Obsessed?

HARRY: Your mother.

CLARE: Did she even care that she was leaving behind a husband with an empty toolbox and a baby?

HARRY: Just because this Shaw guy killed himself you don't know that she did.

CLARE: But –

HARRY: You're dragging some ghost around and that could indicate . . .

CLARE: What, indicate what?

HARRY: That you bought a ticket to the nut house.

CLARE: I don't think I'm traveling alone.

HARRY: Quit acting.

(Beat.)

CLARE: I'm not.

HARRY: Right, and this isn't a drink.

CLARE: Not an actress.

HARRY: You get my Oscar vote. "And our next nominee, in the unforgettable role of a tortured business student searching for her mother's ghost."

CLARE: I did study acting. For a semester. At City College. Before I dropped out.

HARRY: Terrific. So are you getting an MBA or not? Columbia says no. Starbucks says no.

CLARE: Do you have any job openings here?

HARRY: What kind of scam are you running?! You have some deal going with Carlos?

CLARE: I've never met Carlos.

HARRY: That's his story too.

CLARE: There's no scam.

HARRY: Then just what the hell -

CLARE: My attorney told me I needed to make an effort. Plus I had to vacate my apartment.

HARRY: This on top of Daddy dying?

CLARE: Yes.

HARRY: Sure, of course.

CLARE: Last month this man holding an ax crawled through my window, screaming that I had to get out, right now. I didn't argue, not with the ax and all.

HARRY: And I'm the one who's been worried about over the edge.

CLARE:  No really.  He was wearing a helmet that said FDNY.  Across the hall their kitchen was on fire.  The firemen  have these big ladders on their trucks and the one with the ax came through my window and carried me out in his arms.  I took that as a sign.

HARRY:  Your hero had arrived.

CLARE:  No, that guy's never shown up.  My life all of a sudden was a piddly joke and so not going nowhere.  Plus the apartment was now trashed.  Plus plus my drunk dad was now dead.  Anyway that's more or less, I guess more than less, kind of how a storage locker got me searching for my mother's lover from the Bellevue nut ward.  I thought that maybe if I followed his bread crumbs . . . all I had was a letter from Costa Rica.

*(Beat.  HARRY stares at CLARE.)*

CLARE:  Doesn't make a lot of sense, does it?

HARRY:  Don't dig up creatures who can hurt you, who can put you under.

*(LOAN enters unseen.)*

CLARE:  Is it really so weird to want to know who your mother was, why she died?

HARRY:  I can't help you.  I said get out.  Now!

*(HARRY steps toward her with aggression.  CLARE backs up.)*

CLARE:  Not before I give you this.

*(CLARE tosses the object at HARRY.)*

HARRY:  Don't throw shit at me young lady.

*(As HARRY retrieves and unwraps object he notices LOAN.  His gaze bounces between the contents and Loan.  Tries to hide his distress but without success.)*

CLARE:  A Purple Heart.

HARRY: What am I supposed to do with it?

CLARE: Take it back.

HARRY: No one listens around here. *(glances at LOAN)*

CLARE: I came here to see if I could maybe find this Shaw and if I did maybe I could help him and in some weird way help her and in some weirder way help me get my life to start working.

HARRY: *(another glance at LOAN)* You can't help the dead and you may be beyond help.

CLARE: If you're not Harrison Shaw then this isn't yours either.

*(CLARE throws an art auction catalog at HARRY.)*

HARRY: Quit throwing shit.

CLARE: Guess what else I found, you know, in the locker? Five paintings, that's what. They couldn't buy her a subway token but over the years their value has gone up. *(points to the catalog)* There's one in there named "Triage". It sold this summer for eighty-eight thousand dollars. Taped to the back was a note on Bellevue stationary. *(reads that note)* "For Harrison, whose kindness made the brushes move again." Signed Virginia Easton, October sixteen, nineteen sixty-nine. The day before she died. My attorney said I had to make an effort to find Shaw before I could spend that money.

HARRY: If this Shaw didn't off himself or kill her and you can find him then he's a lucky bastard. That hardly fits my profile.

CLARE: So should I just head back and spend that money?

HARRY: Yes. Get a nice apartment, on the ground floor, with a smoke detector. . . . You should be careful.

CLARE: Why?

HARRY: Maybe this Shaw did have something to do with your mother's death. Maybe he's a twisted fuck just looking for someone to pay for all the shit that's come his way.

CLARE: Where did someone who knows Latin learn to talk like that?

HARRY: In a jungle.

CLARE: You're not in the jungle here.

HARRY: Think not? Maybe you're sloshing through a paddy with snipers all around.

CLARE: I'll take my chances. . . But just in case, there's an attorney on upper Broadway with instructions to open a letter if I'm not back by Monday.

HARRY: At least you read detective novels.

CLARE: I just want to know the truth.

HARRY: History's a mystery.

CLARE: The way my mother wrote about Shaw in her diary made me even wonder if he could be my father.

HARRY: Come on!

CLARE: Don't worry, don't worry, I figured out that was impossible, the dates don't work. She would have had to fly to Saigon for a weekend fling. So Paul Gutterman was my excuse for a father.

*(Long beat. HARRY makes a questioning gesture to LOAN. CLARE is confused by his gesture. LOAN nods assent. HARRY gestures for CLARE to turn her head to profile. At first she doesn't understand what he wants, then gets it, turns her head.)*

HARRY: You, the way your smile turns up at the corner, yeah, that's it.

CLARE: That's it what?

HARRY: Her lips, her happy-sad smile. You have it.

CLARE: *(sigh of relief)* Does that make me a ghost?

HARRY: *(anger gone, now relieved)* Sure, why not, the more the merrier. . . Virginia, she was so kind, so good, and she was injured. She had a heart as big as the South China Sea. She breathed life into my dead bones. She saved me when I wasn't worth saving. I tried to save her.

CLARE: Did you love my mother?

HARRY: Ohhh, a tiger stepping out of bamboo could not have sent my heart racing any faster. Do you know how beautiful she was?

CLARE: I have pictures but no, not like that beautiful. I hope someone, that someone loves me like that some day.

HARRY: Be careful what you wish for. Windows with padded bars, doors that don't lock, crayons to write with, more meds than we could count - that's hardly solid ground. Who really knows if what we had would have survived that winter?

CLARE: Did she ever say anything about me?

HARRY: The biggest reason she wanted to get better was so she could take care of you. Her smile, your smile, it's not simple. I'm not saying it's Mona Lisa but it's a complicated smile.

CLARE: How did she die? I need to know.

RIMBAUD THE PARROT: What we imagine -

HARRY: *(to RIMBAUD)* Hola amigo.

RIMBAUD THE PARROT: knowledge to be. Dark, salt, clear -

HARRY: *(to CLARE)* It's ugly. *(to RIMBAUD)* Good.

*(HARRY takes a moment to give RIMBAUD a food treat.)*

HARRY: *(to CLARE)* That's his hardest one.

CLARE: I can take it.

HARRY: I'm not so sure either of us . . . *(takes deep breath)* Okay, as Rimbaud says, knowledge. Your mother liked her cigarettes, Camel filters, but we couldn't smoke on the ward. One night this orderly snuck her up onto the roof for a smoke. She had been real low that day. Another patient saw them leave and when they didn't come back he got a bad feeling and followed them. The orderly had her on the ground, one hand over her mouth, the other hand ripping her pants. This patient tried to pull the orderly off, all three were fighting, she was screaming. The patient kicked him, they were near the edge, the orderly started to fall, he grabbed her ankle and they both went over. Just like that. That's how life ends. *(clicks fingers)* A hair sliver cracks in time and we slip through. No rhyme, reason, crack, slip, lights out.

CLARE: Oh my god. That's really how she died? How horrible! So she didn't - [kill herself?]

HARRY: No, she was a fighter. That's really how she died.

CLARE: Oh my god. Oh no. She was a really good painter. That's what they tell me in New York. They say she could have been great. Shit. What kind of mother do you think she would have been?

HARRY: The best.

CLARE: You think so.

HARRY: I more than think so.

CLARE: The other patient, him, what happened to him?

HARRY: Ran down the fire escape, saw they were both goners, closed her eyes, and fled.

CLARE: Where?

HARRY: *(beat)* South.

CLARE: How'd he know they were dead?

HARRY: That patient had zipped up a lot of body bags.

CLARE: *(she gets it)* When he was a medic in Vietnam.

HARRY: Corpsman. Stuffed with boys who might have - [lived] . . . if he had had more skill and less fear.

CLARE: Holy shit, holy shit, that's so . . . so that's . . . What a waste; for both of you. Why Costa Rica?

HARRY: Stopped for a cup of coffee and stayed to grow the beans. A country without an army did hold a certain appeal. He was sick - sick of war, sick of Vietnam, sick of himself, sick of America, sick of death. That's enough questions.

CLARE: Okay. . . But why did you quit poetry?

HARRY: Come on. It quit me. Wasted and wounded. Whatever pond that fountain flowed from, the war pretty much dried it up.

CLARE: So you found a rock called Costa Rica and crawled under it.

HARRY: You go fight in a useless war, any war, Hannibal or Ho in Hanoi, doesn't matter, and then talk to me about a rock. I arrived here with no tomorrow, one leg and half a mind, maybe half a mind. I just wanted to get far, far away and be alone. Fuck poetry, fuck America, fuck family.

CLARE: Excuse me, have you looked around here lately?

HARRY: A roomful of ghosts and a farm that's going under.

CLARE: The family bit.

HARRY: What?

CLARE: You need eye surgery.

HARRY: You have your story. Go fit that into your puzzle. You're dismissed.

CLARE: Center stage we have a depressed farmer who drinks way too much, along with his parrot. And what else? A brilliant boy who worships him, who he's taught some language spoken by really old guys, and over here we have a beautiful woman devoted to you who has helped raise your son and kept you from falling apart. I don't know Spanish so I'm not sure what they call this in Costa Rica but back home this looks a hell of a lot like a family. I think you're full of crap Harry Howell or Harrison Shaw or whoever you are. You say my mother cared about me -

HARRY: She did.

CLARE: - but I never knew that. You've got a lot more family than I ever had. Do you see how much Dora loves you? Who knows what Javier's going to achieve? You are so blind. You've created a masterpiece here.

HARRY: Right, Gauguin in paradise, that's me.

CLARE: Her painting, the money from it, I know it's not enough to save the farm but from what Dora told me it can keep you going for another month or two. And by then coffee prices could -

HARRY: Go up? Hmmf.

CLARE: Possible.

HARRY: Not the way Vietnam's flooding the market. West of Saigon, near the Cambodian border, we came into a hostile village one day and went to see the chief. Hanging on the wall above him was the holy trinity. On the right, Comrade Lenin. On the left, Herr Marx. And in the middle, the native prophet Uncle Ho. Now look at Vietnam. What were we so afraid of? I should have been worried about their coffee, not their politics.

CLARE: Have you ever gone back?

HARRY: I don't think so.

CLARE: Why not?

HARRY: What do you think of a dog who eats his own vomit?

CLARE:  It's a tragedy you had to go in the first place.

HARRY:  Didn't.

CLARE:  Didn't?

HARRY:  Didn't have to.

CLARE:  You weren't drafted?

HARRY:  'fraid not.  I was bored with school and had always loved The Iliad.

CLARE:  I don't -

HARRY:  It's a book where the hero Achilles is promised glory or a long life. Sorry, can't have both.  Harrison Shaw was a foolish boy who went for the glory. . . . but then the gods betrayed him.

CLARE:  How?

HARRY:  They dealt him long life instead.  At least this long.

CLARE:  You went to war because of some guy in a book?

HARRY:  Achilles is not just some guy.  And you gotta watch out for those books. Not my best decision.  Take care with yours.

CLARE:  I'm trying to get better at them.

HARRY:  That's not obvious.  You can never know.

CLARE:  Never know what?

*(HARRY becomes disoriented, looks at the Purple Heart and Loan.)*

HARRY:  Where those waves will carry your boat.  You just never know.  That morning maybe her mother was going to take her along to the market to sell a chicken and at the last minute she changed her mind and decided to stay in the village, to sell the chicken another day.

RIMBAUD THE PARROT: Squawk.

HARRY: *(to CLARE)* The chicken's a distant cousin.

CLARE: I don't understand.

HARRY: I don't either. It wasn't a friendly visit.

*(Birds are singing in the background.)*

CLARE: Do you get many visitors?

HARRY: Have you seen any?

CLARE: No, should I?

HARRY: I don't know.

CLARE: Visitors from America, do you ever get any?

HARRY: Except for the buyers trying to beat me up on price and phony business students, the only ones I see are those with feathers.

CLARE: Feathers?

HARRY: Three months ago they were chirping in Ohio or Connecticut. America wears them out. *(beat)* Lately I miss the snow. The way it falls soft and paints the branches white and hits your face and when the wind kicks up your cheeks can tingle.

CLARE: It was snowing when I left New York. When I get back I'll send you a cashier's check. I really will.

HARRY: Can I see the book?

CLARE: Be careful, you gotta watch out for those books.

*(CLARE hands HARRY book.)*

CLARE:  You can keep it.

HARRY:  What time's your plane leave?

CLARE:  Four.  Maybe I'll fly back down some winter and check in with you.

HARRY:  My farm may not be here.

CLARE:  Your family will be.  I could come back sooner if you have a job opening.

HARRY:  Don't count on it.  I may be looking for a job myself.

*(Beat.)*

CLARE:  Or we may not ever see each other again.  Can I . . . would it be all right if I, if we . . . ?

*(Awkwardness.  CLARE extends her arms to offer a hug.  She hugs HARRY and he responds partway.)*


## ACT 2, SCENE 2

*(That evening, Saturday.  LOAN observes DORA and HARRY.)*

HARRY:  You're in a shitty mood.  The rain getting to you?

DORA:  That must be it . . . maybe I'm worried we're going to run into problems.  Do you think? *(turns serious)* Carlos is trying to rob you.

HARRY:  I'm hardly negotiating from a position of strength.

DORA:  You only nibbled at your breakfast.

HARRY:  I'm not hungry, and anyway I'm cutting back on the meat.

*(HARRY gestures "See?" to LOAN.  DORA doesn't notice.)*

DORA:  Whatever for?

HARRY:  A doctor advised it.

DORA:  Go on, you haven't seen a doctor in years, except for your leg.  Get your priorities straight: quit the cigarettes, cut the vodka in half, then maybe worry about meat.

HARRY:  Let me worry about me.  You help worry about the farm.

DORA:  Where were you last night?

HARRY:  In the barn.  I read til I dozed off, around three.

DORA:  Our bed has forgotten what you look like.

HARRY:  Our eyes, when we die our eyes, they're the same size as when we are born.  Did you know that?

DORA:  No.

HARRY:  The eyes don't —

*(HARRY struggles to articulate "grow"; finally gets it out.  His speech problem worries DORA.)*

HARRY:  grow.  When a kid looks like he has big eyes, well he sort of does, but it's only because his skull is so small and that's going to keep growing.  But the eye sockets, they got the ants going.  It makes sense that if the eyes don't — grow, the eye sockets don't either.  Otherwise an eye'd end up looking look like, what, some coffee bean staring out of a salad bowl?

DORA:  Are eyes what's tying your tongue and keeping you awake?

HARRY:  Well it's all confusing.

DORA:  What is?

HARRY:  This eye ball, eye socket thing.  Kids have such big eyes.

DORA:  Did you see her during the night?

HARRY:  *(glances at LOAN)* Did you?

DORA:  Not after I fixed the couch.

HARRY:  Oh.  I poked my head in and saw she was sound asleep.  Then I went to the barn.

DORA:  This morning you smelled like a goat, way worse than Javi's shoes.

HARRY:  *(makes goat sounds)*

DORA:  She asks such a lot of questions.  But I guess if she's going to get a job at Starbucks, and all the top guns are going to read her whatever, you can't very well tell her to get lost.

HARRY:  Listen, the truth is, she's already lost.

DORA:  What?

HARRY:  Big-time, major-league lost.  She's not who she says she is.  When I was young her mother and I were in love and now thirty years later this girl has somehow tracked me down.

DORA:  Wow.  Why?

HARRY:  Looking for answers.  Her mother -

DORA:  *(connects the dots)* The artist woman.

HARRY:  That's right, a terrific painter who — died way too young in this weird tragic way and no one really knows exactly what happened. . . .

DORA:  Except you?

HARRY:  That's right, except — me.

DORA:  Harry, you didn't -

HARRY: No I did not! I tried to save her but saving people, that's not my strong suit.

DORA: So no mother, no father, and no job at Starbucks.

HARRY: That's a lot of no's. But she doesn't need to worry about a job right away. She recently came into some money, or so she says.

DORA: Lost with money, hmmm.

HARRY: Her mother left me some money too, or at least a painting that sold for money, that's what Clare says.

DORA: How much money?

HARRY: Eighty-eight thousand dollars.

DORA: Really!? Do you believe her?

HARRY: I kinda think so.

DORA: Well isn't that something? Wow; eighty-eight thousand?

HARRY: That's what she says.

DORA: Last night, in the middle of the night, I woke up. Went and got a blanket.

HARRY: It got cold. I should have come back in and closed the windows. *(overcome by fear of failure)* I don't know if we're going to make it, even with her money, if that's for real. I don't know if I'm going to make it.

DORA: I don't either. Is there more than the farm - and those eyeballs in the salad bowl - bothering you?

HARRY: *(glances at LOAN)* And now some crazy girl hunting me down.

DORA: But also maybe bringing you money. What's that?

*(DORA points to a bit of purple ribbon visible in HARRY's fist.)*

HARRY: Something she brought with her, of her mother's, that used to be mine.

*(HARRY hands DORA the Purple Heart medal.)*

DORA: Yours?

HARRY: Was. I tried to leave it in America. It's what the government gives you when you lose a leg. I was a soldier once, in Vietnam.

DORA: Harry, you gotta get straight with me.

HARRY: Don't start in!

DORA: This can't go on.

HARRY: Tell me! I'm exhausted. The enemy has way too many soldiers. I can't fight them all, not anymore. I try to take care of you and Javi and I'm not - [getting the job done].

*(DORA goes to comfort HARRY. He resists at first then allows DORA into his space.)*

HARRY: Do you believe in ghosts?

DORA: Do you?

HARRY: I believe that whatever we are, maybe it doesn't stop at the skin. Our eyes tell us we stop at the skin but I don't think that's true.

*(HARRY touches DORA.)*

HARRY: You don't stop at your skin, not for me.

DORA: I believe in Harry Howell. Even if he has been looking like a ghost. Don't ask me why; not this month.

HARRY: No seriously, do you?

DORA: Sure. Ghosts are spirits who are lost and can't get home.

HARRY: Like they're missing some kind of visa?

DORA: Something like that.

HARRY: Where is home?

DORA: You're the one who takes Javi to Mass every week. Where we all want to go. Heaven. To be with our Savior, His Father, and the Blessed Mother.

*(DORA kisses HARRY on the forehead. He looks up at her. She gives him a quick kiss on the mouth.)*

DORA: I got really cold last night.

HARRY: So you -

*(DORA doesn't let HARRY finish. She kisses him more deeply. For a moment he responds, then the flame goes out.)*

HARRY: I'm sorry, it's just no good.

DORA: You are not well mi gordo. There is only one true medicine and you won't take it. You forget, yo por ti y tu por mi.

*(DORA picks up a stick-like object and makes mock sword thrusts at HARRY.)*

HARRY: *(musters a smile)* Me for you and you for me. Who'll be our third musketeer?

DORA: Javi of course.

HARRY: That's right, Javi. "The best my boy" -

DORA: "the bravest."

HARRY: He's old enough now for a sword and a cape, maybe even one of those feathered caps.

DORA:  Rimbaud can chip in the feather.

RIMBAUD THE PARROT:  Squawk.

DORA:  See?

HARRY:  This farm, it's sucked up my years faster than the dirt soaks up the rain. . . If you were me would you even want to look in the m— mirror?

DORA:  What?

HARRY:  Look.  And if you did, what would you see?

DORA:  Go on.

HARRY:  Could you keep your food down?

DORA:  Stop it!  Don't talk like this.

HARRY:  You should bury me and marry someone younger.

DORA:  Someone nicer anyway.

HARRY:  You still have time.

DORA:  Time for what?

HARRY:  To have a family.

DORA:  I do have a family, a little crazy maybe.

HARRY:  You do?

DORA:  Look here, in my eyes.  Maybe eyes don't get bigger but that's not true for what's in here. *(points to her heart)* My heart has swelled to hold you and Javi and even this whole farm.  Come on!, you're not looking.  You can be such a fool.

HARRY:  You should get out.

DORA: You want to push me out, don't you?

HARRY: I'm trying to look after you.

DORA: You can't even look after yourself.

HARRY: You deserve someone better.

DORA: You're damned right I do!  This is bullshit Harry.  You know when a man vomits this crap?  When he wants to leave a woman.  Is there someone else?

*(HARRY and LOAN exchange a quick glance.)*

RIMBAUD THE PARROT: Squawk.

HARRY: You shut up!

*(JAVIER enters, sheepishly because he has heard the yelling.)*

HARRY: What do you want?

JAVIER: Well I'm working on my chemistry homework and I can't find my calculator.  Do you think I can borrow yours tonight?

HARRY: Go ahead and get out.  But you better find yours.  We already spent money on new shoes.

RIMBAUD THE PARROT: Squawk.

HARRY: What'd I say?!

DORA: I spent my money on new shoes, so you hush about that.  Javi, can you please tell us who is it that's been a complete total pain in the ass around here the last month?

JAVIER: Umm, I'd really rather not say.

HARRY: Smart boy.  Go do your homework.

*(JAVIER exits, glad to escape.)*

DORA: Keep this up and I will be gone. Javi too. You can be all by yourself and have vodka for breakfast, lunch and dinner. Then one night I'll get a call asking me to come back here and bury you. Do you ever think about me?

HARRY: Yes, I -

DORA: Like shit you do. Your heart hasn't grown; it's shrunk. I doubt that it's even this big. *(holds up medal and throws it at him)* I can't take this much longer.

*(DORA starts to leave. HARRY retrieves medal.)*

HARRY: That's it; you're leaving?

DORA: That's what you just told me to do.

HARRY: No I didn't.

DORA: Arghhhh!

*(DORA storms out.)*

LOAN: You are a lucky man.

HARRY: Right, just full of fucking luck.

LOAN: She is right.

HARRY: She always thinks she is right.

LOAN: About the one true medicine.

HARRY: So you're a doctor too?

LOAN: You were the corpsman. I only knew my mother's love. But other women in my world have told me about these things. . . Javier is very handsome.

HARRY: You stay away from him.

LOAN: Don't worry, no mortal can feel the touch of a ghost. . . Has he enjoyed a woman yet?

HARRY: That's not information a son shares with his father.

LOAN: Is that a great pleasure?

HARRY: Yeah. For the young especially. The Earth can move.

LOAN: Around the sun? Like Copernicus?

HARRY: No. The ground just shivers a bit.

LOAN: *(confused)* The Earth?

HARRY: Never mind. It keeps the species going.

LOAN: And for you?

HARRY: For me what?

LOAN: Does the Earth move for you?

HARRY: Not anymore. Just ask Dora.

LOAN: The women, the women in my world, they smile about these things, and sometimes they tease me. With Dora the gods have blessed you.

HARRY: Is that right?

LOAN: It is. Hold her close. Kiss her tears. Take her medicine.

HARRY: Who are you?! Some sort of avenging angel? Or the Asian Hallucination?

LOAN: More ghost than angel.

HARRY: You need to help me here with the celestial taxonomy. Just how much difference can there be?

LOAN:  As much as between Greek and Latin.  Angels live in palaces and they have more power.  Ghosts have no  residence; we are in transit, traveling over an abyss with no passport.  Angels can cry - too often in my opinion - we can't.  And those wings.  Angels get those fabulous designer wings.  We hate them for their big white wings.

HARRY:  Wings?

LOAN:  *(snarky)* Tell me they really need that many feathers?

HARRY:  How would - [I know?]

LOAN:  Vanity.  That's what we say.

HARRY:  How much longer will this, this go on?

LOAN:  Until you don't need me.

HARRY:  Why do I need you?

LOAN:  I told you -

HARRY:  Do you see the future?

LOAN:  Like bamboo in the fog across a rice paddy.

HARRY:  Dangerous conditions.  You said the sh — shore's not far away.

LOAN:  Already I've said too much.  We're not supposed to talk about these things.

HARRY:  Why?

LOAN:  Misunderstanding is too easy.

HARRY:  So here I am, teetering, toes gripping the edge, maybe, maybe talking with a ghost who's worried about misunderstanding.  What is wrong with this picture?  Carlos is right, isn't he?  I'm losing it, I am losing it big time.

LOAN: If I were having problems upstairs, Carlos wouldn't be the first person I'd go to. If I say you won't see the sun tomorrow, you'll expect death but I may just be forecasting heavy fog.

HARRY: Hiding bamboo across the paddy. I got medals for sloshing through those paddies, pulling off leeches, dodging bullets.

*(Long beat.)*

LOAN: And attacking villages. I know Harry. . . Mother was lying -

HARRY: Mother?

LOAN: She knew where Father was on that most terrible of days when your marines came to our village. Look in your hand.

*(HARRY looks at medal and LOAN.)*

HARRY: So that's who you really are; you're that girl?

*(HARRY reaches to touch LOAN. LOAN reacts with slight aggression and moves out of his reach.)*

HARRY: I can see you, her, I mean if that's who you really are. Screaming your lungs out. All that sn —

*(HARRY can't get the word out, finally makes motion indicating a flow from the nose.)*

LOAN: Snot you call it.

HARRY: Down your chin. Those red shorts, all muddy, light rain coming down, your big eyes. What am I saying? I can see you now. I'm seeing you now, aren't I? Am I? *(trying to maintain equilibrium)* Shit! Just where the hell do you come from!? I really don't like what I'm seeing.

LOAN: I don't either.

HARRY: Ha! And the little dog laughed to see such sport.

LOAN: No -

HARRY: And the dish ran away with the spoon. Wait a minute, wait. . . . Just how did your mother lie?

LOAN: *(angry)* How? To protect her family! You don't remember?! Mother was screaming at you!: Giet toi di nhung dung ham hai con gai toi. Khong! Khong! Dung dung den con gai toi. Oi troi oi! Oi con gai toi! Oi troi oi! *(beat to catch her breath)*

HARRY: Where is your mother now?

LOAN: She suffered, died and moved on.

HARRY: And your father?

LOAN: Killed in battle a week after I was murdered. Father really was Viet Cong, and mother did know where they were hiding.

HARRY: Where?

LOAN: Right underneath us.

HARRY: Huh?

LOAN: There were tunnels.

HARRY: Those fuckers. So we were right?

LOAN: You were so fucking wrong. You were an invader during a civil war. Expected rain, got caught in a monsoon that spurted blood for ten years.

HARRY: Is that what we do, I mean after the fighting and the suffering and the dying - we "move on"?

LOAN: When steel sliced my neck mother placed a curse on you.

HARRY: But I didn't -

LOAN: The machete wasn't in your fist but -

HARRY: She was attacking him.

LOAN: Hah! While clutching a screaming girl!

HARRY: I tried to stop him.

LOAN: No, Corpsman Shaw, I'm sorry, all you did was stare. Mother was shielding me like a bird covering her baby with a wing.

RIMBAUD THE PARROT: Squawk.

LOAN: *(glancing at RIMBAUD)* He knows.

HARRY: No he doesn't.

LOAN: You think he's just Harry's little parrot? Don't be a fool. You just stared, a silent coward staring.

HARRY: No, no, no, that's not what I - [remember]

LOAN: Yes, yes, yes; coffee grows in snow better than soldiers remember battle.

HARRY: Land mines had just vaporized two of our men. They were unbottled spiders with fangs bubbling.

LOAN: You were the only one there sane enough to save me.

HARRY: You're charging me with sanity!

LOAN: You just stood there.

HARRY: I couldn't stop marines gone berserk.

LOAN: She grew old, a war widow, no daughter to hold her hand, no grandchildren to tickle.

HARRY: Ever since your village, that day in your village, I have carried you with me, a heavy, sweaty pack across three decades. I have a hole in here that your eyes drilled out. So deep and so fucking empty.

LOAN: Admit you blew it Harry.

HARRY: Any idea how crazy, I mean really fucking crazy, this all is? Your eyes. It was war I tell you; you were collateral damage.

LOAN: The gods favored mother's curse.

HARRY: Right, of course they did. And those whom the gods destroy, they — first make mad. You bet. *(looks upward and shouts)* Go ahead you bastards, enjoy your fucking games! *(unbalanced laughter)* How cr — crazy is that?

LOAN: What?

HARRY: That there's someone up there who gives a shit about us? Now that's crazy.

*(A Buddhist chant, "Namo Amitabha Buddha," begins in background. HARRY becomes alarmed. Chant subsides after a few moments.)*

HARRY: What's that? What is that?

LOAN: Prayers.

HARRY: For whom?

LOAN: You, me too. You hold my visa.

HARRY: And where's mine? Where do you need to go?

LOAN: I ache to be alive again. The last time got cut short, remember?

HARRY: You realize there's no safe landing zone, that pain and grief grow faster than elephant grass.

LOAN: I'm tired of being stuck.

HARRY: So is this the bit where I get three wishes but lacking imagination I blow it and am damned forever?

LOAN: One wish.

HARRY: Just one?

LOAN: Just one. And you don't even deserve that.

HARRY: Why did you pick last month to show up?

LOAN: I've never been far away.

HARRY: But last - [month]

LOAN: You were going to need me.

HARRY: Is there really a river there -

RIMBAUD THE PARROT: Dark, salt, clear -

HARRY: where you come from, where if you go in it you can forget to remember? And there's this weird dog hanging around?

LOAN: *(playing)* I can't remember. I think I forget.

*(HARRY is not amused.)*

LOAN: I haven't seen it but others tell me stories. I like to remember my mother, the smell of her skin, her lips nuzzling my neck, how she peeled papaya, the songs she sang. A daughter wants to hear her mother sing, even if the songs are sad. . . I came here to help you.

HARRY: You really did?

LOAN: Come on Harry. I'm like some taxi driver who's keeping the meter running. "But when thou shalt be old, thou shalt stretch forth thy hands, and another shall gird thee, and carry thee whither thou wouldst not."

HARRY:  A Buddhist taxi driver with a Bible and no passport.  Where's the Thorazine when you really need it? . . . There's a storm coming isn't there?  I can smell it.

LOAN:  Our journeys were joined in my village.

HARRY:  Where there was a girl and a mother and fire and rain and blood all over. How did Heaven tie us together?

LOAN:  When you came into my village a string was plucked that's never stopped vibrating.  When our suffering is done -

HARRY:  It gets done?

LOAN:  We can each get going.

HARRY:  But where, how . . .


## ACT 2, SCENE 3

*(Next day, Sunday morning.  Raining.  HARRY and JAVIER have recently returned from 8:00 Mass in Grecia.  HARRY looks out the window.  DORA enters with a plate of cookies.)*

HARRY:  Hey there.  You've been busy.  Looks good.

*(HARRY takes a cookie.)*

DORA:  What happened to you last night?

HARRY:  What?

DORA:  The barn didn't miss you?

HARRY:  Somehow I think the goats got through the night just fine.

DORA:  Plus this morning you smelled a lot better.

HARRY: I slept like a baby.

DORA: I noticed. I dreamed about a tiger.

HARRY: You did?

DORA: Um-hmm.

HARRY: Was he on your tail?

DORA: Um-hmm.

HARRY: Did he catch you?

DORA: Um-hmm.

HARRY: So it was a nightmare.

DORA: Nuh-uh, not at all. I hadn't seen that tiger for a long time. I was sweaty and then we fell asleep. Later a breeze came with the rain but the tiger kept me warm.

HARRY: We've kept each other warm for a lot of years.

*(DORA kisses HARRY as JAVIER enters.)*

DORA: *(to JAVIER, holding up cookies)* Guess what happened while you were at Mass?

JAVIER: *(diving for them)* Ummm, butter cookies. You haven't made these for a while.

DORA: *(smiling at JAVIER)* Save a few for Harry.

HARRY: *(to DORA)* Thank you.

JAVIER: *(with a mouthful; to DORA)* Yeah, thank you.

*(DORA exits.)*

HARRY: You could barely hear the Padre because of his cold.

JAVIER: It's going around. We were short on altar boys because so many are sick.

HARRY: The Padre's sermon, what we could hear of it, what did you think it was about?

JAVIER: It's important to keep your house in order here so you can live with God in Heaven.

HARRY: *(goes to window and looks up)* Yes, something like that. The rain's letting up, at least for a minute anyway.

JAVIER: Why don't you ever go up for Communion?

HARRY: *(spying a hawk in the sky)* I eat before we go. When you see the hawk high above the coffee, do you think you can grow up like him and soar anywhere you want?

JAVIER: No.

HARRY: No?

JAVIER: Not really.

HARRY: Why not?

JAVIER: Don't know.

HARRY: What do you think?

JAVIER: I'm thinking there's a mouse in that field who better watch out.

HARRY: Smart boy. That soaring hawk stuff may only be what an old man imagines he once felt. Maybe the hawk was just a sparrow. How does Latin sound this afternoon, say around three o'clock?

JAVIER: All right.

HARRY: It's a deal. We'll work our way through that rough patch of Cicero -

*(LOAN enters. HARRY sees her, making him nervous.)*

HARRY: Have I ever told you about my will?

JAVIER: No.

HARRY: If anything ever happens to me, you and Dora need go to my lawyer. Name is Martinez; office on Calle Dagaz in Grecia. Dora has met him.

JAVIER: *(taken aback)* Okay.

HARRY: Yeah?

JAVIER: I understand.

HARRY: Martinez on Calle Dagaz.

JAVIER: I got it.

HARRY: Don't worry, I'm feeling okay for a one-legged old fart. I just want you and Dora to know there's a will and where it is. I'm responsible for you, right?

JAVIER: I guess.

HARRY: Still leaning toward medicine?

JAVIER: Yeah. And I'm acing chemistry this term.

HARRY: I want you to graduate from university before you get serious with any girl. Okay?

JAVIER: You already -

HARRY: It's okay to taste the candy but you don't buy the store 'til after university.

JAVIER: *(smiling)* Right, okay. . . How would a Roman say that?

HARRY:  Taberna.

JAVIER:  Not store, the other.

HARRY:  What other?

JAVIER:  *(sheepish smile)* You know.

HARRY:  *(teasing him)* No I don't.

JAVIER:  Yes you do.

HARRY:  No I don't.

JAVIER:  You do so.

HARRY:  Sorry.

JAVIER:  Come on.  You know, the candy stuff.

HARRY:  Ohhh, the candy stuff; how did a Roman say taste the candy?

JAVIER:  Yeah.

HARRY:  Misceo.

JAVIER:  Third conjugation?

HARRY:  El segundo.  Don't worry Javi, you'll have plenty of time to learn that verb.

*(CARLOS enters.)*

CARLOS:  Hi.  Dora let me in.  That rain's nasty.

HARRY:  We know.  It's a mudpile out there.

CARLOS:  What's going on?  Not supposed to rain in December.  Hello Javier. It's been years.  How are you?

HARRY: You remember Carlos?

JAVIER: A little. Fine thank you.

CARLOS: You're hardly the boy anymore. Harry's very proud of you. I can see why. *(to HARRY)* You've got a problem in a ditch. I drove in the back way and a truck is on its side.

HARRY: Where?

CARLOS: The main ditch on the east edge of the farm. Two boys are with it. They said no one was hurt. But they're not going to get that truck out by themselves.

HARRY: Javi, I have to meet with Carlos now. Go get the tractor and help those boys pull out their truck.

*(JAVIER looks out the window, searching for an excuse.)*

JAVIER: It's starting to come down again.

HARRY: Yes I see that. But I also see problems if that truck leaks fuel into our ditches. Grab a raincoat. The sooner you get going, the sooner you'll be back.

JAVIER: Ohhhh.

HARRY: Go on. Get going.

CARLOS: You can't miss it. It's an old black Ford.

HARRY: Grab that thick rope to take with you. On the wall next to the tractor.

*(JAVIER exits.)*

HARRY: Take a seat.

*(BOTH sit.)*

HARRY: Thanks for coming by again.

CARLOS: Not a problem. So, how many offers have you had since yesterday?

HARRY:  I was giving you the courtesy of not speaking to others until we finished.

CARLOS:  Thank you.

*(HARRY picks up Clare's auction catalog and drops it on desk.)*

HARRY:  In the meantime you never know, some angel could fly in and drop a pot of gold on the farm.

CARLOS:  Just make sure you're not standing under it.  I've been thinking, I would be willing to go up another half million per hectare.

HARRY:  Well -

CARLOS:  And no more talk of robbery.  Think about it for more than a minute and you'll realize that where coffee prices are - and there's no sign they're turning around anytime soon - I'm being generous.  It'd give you enough to pay off the mortgage.

HARRY:  How do you know the balance on my mortgage?

CARLOS:  Educated guess, that's all.

HARRY:  What you don't know about me is a lot.

CARLOS:  And I'm thinking you've got stuff in there I don't want to know.

HARRY:  I don't really come from America.

CARLOS:  So just where then?

HARRY:  War.

*(CARLOS doesn't know what to say.)*

HARRY:  War.

CARLOS:  Oh that's right, where the elephant stepped on your leg.

HARRY:  A man with one leg can be dangerous.

CARLOS:  Because the wooden one can be a club?

HARRY:  He has less to lose.  I was conceived in mud, I spent nine months in battle, war spread its legs, cocked its knees and shot Harry H—Howell into the world.  I was baptized in the Mekong not the Mississippi.  I'm a creature of war.

CARLOS:  In the may-what?  You need to go home man.

HARRY:  I am home.  But that's probably where you should go if you're not serious.

CARLOS:  Not serious?  Come on Harry, cut the shit, what am I doing here listening to your dribble on a Sunday morning, raising my offer by half a million?

*(CARLOS starts to leave.)*

HARRY:  Maybe I don't need to sell now.

CARLOS:  Oh, did coffee prices suddenly go up overnight?  You need a doctor, not a buyer.  You're not well.

HARRY:  I'm all right.

CARLOS:  Have you looked in the mirror lately?  You're a mess.  Not fucking well at all.

HARRY:  You don't know how hard I've worked to build up this farm.

CARLOS:  I hate to break the news but how hard you've worked  has nothing to do with what your farm's worth today.  Nothing. You might as well start calling other farmers to see if they're interested.

HARRY:  I w—will.

CARLOS:  Go right ahead, be a fool.

HARRY:  Don't start b-being a jerk.

CARLOS:  Right.  Who's *(mimicking)* b-b-being a j-j-j-jerk here?

HARRY:  Fuck off Carlos!

CARLOS:  No, you fuck off.  Is this all it takes to push you over the edge?

RIMBAUD THE PARROT:  Vigil strange I kept -

HARRY:  *(to RIMBAUD)* Shut up!

*(CARLOS thinks "Shut up!" is directed at him.)*

RIMBAUD THE PARROT:  - on the field one night.

*(HARRY loses control of his anger, yanks water pistol from drawer. CARLOS, positioned in the same direction as RIMBAUD, thinks HARRY has a real gun and intends to shoot him.  CARLOS pulls a pistol he had hidden and goes to shoot HARRY.  HARRY sees CARLOS's gun and at the last possible instant -)*

HARRY:  The parrot you fucking idiot.  I was shooting him.

*(CARLOS points his pistol upward.  HARRY points his pistol at his own temple and squirts water on his head.  They laugh as they realize what almost happened.  CARLOS puts away his pistol.)*

HARRY:  I was squirting the fucking parrot.

CARLOS:  You need to get rid of that parrot before someone gets killed.

HARRY:  *(gestures toward Carlos's gun)* What are you doing with that?

CARLOS:  Same as you; it shuts things up.

HARRY:  Yes. . . It's snowing in Buffalo.

CARLOS:  I suppose it is.  And don't forget the doctor.  Be sure to tell him about the elephants.  I've got to go.

*(CARLOS exits.)*

## ACT 2, SCENE 4

*(Fifteen minutes later. HARRY alone except for LOAN observing him, unseen. Commotion off. The tractor has rolled over in the mud and crushed Javier, who has been brought back to the house and is near death. DORA enters distraught.)*

HARRY: What's going on?  What's wrong?  What's happened!?

*(HARRY moves toward commotion. DORA hurries him toward door.)*

DORA:  It's horrible, an accident, the brakes, they failed, the tractor rolled -

HARRY:  Get out of my way!

*(HARRY exits. Returns carrying JAVIER who is barely conscious. Lays him on the floor.)*

HARRY:  The blanket!

*(DORA brings blanket, they cover JAVIER.)*

HARRY:  Give me room!

*(HARRY begins CPR.)*

HARRY:  *(remembering his corpsman training)* Clear the airway.  Stop the bleeding. Treat for shock.  Clear the airway.  Stop the bleeding.  Treat for shock.

*(HARRY competently treats JAVIER. Despite his efforts he is losing Javier. HARRY is frantic. His mind retreats to Vietnam.)*

HARRY:  Corpsman up!  Corpsman up!  Corpsman up!

*(As Javier's life fades a helicopter's wop-wop sounds rise then recede, as if Javier's soul is leaving on the helicopter. HARRY remembers that Loan has granted him one wish, looks at her to redeem it. But his mind is slipping and he can't get words out. DORA shakes HARRY but his tongue is locked.)*

DORA:  HARRY, DO SOMETHING!

RIMBAUD THE PARROT: *(a shriek such as he's never made before)* SHRIEK!

*(Dora's command plus Rimbaud's shriek snap HARRY back to reality.)*

HARRY: *(to LOAN)* I WANT IT, NOW!

DORA: *(fearing that Harry's mind is slipping further)* Harry!

*(HARRY regains hope; resumes CPR with mouth-to-mouth resuscitation. LOAN goes to them and makes a motion. Helicopter sounds return, low ascending to loud, then landing. JAVIER revives. HARRY realizes JAVIER is alive. Adjusts blankets around JAVIER's shoulders in a sort of hug. DORA is with them.)*

HARRY: That bird almost picked us up.

JAVIER: Bird?

HARRY: Maybe an angel kept it away.

RIMBAUD THE PARROT: *(softly)* Squawk.

JAVIER: Maybe.

HARRY: It won't be long before it comes back for me.

JAVIER: No -

HARRY: Shhh. A soldier with no father tried to be a father. You could have had a better one.

JAVIER: I -

HARRY: but there could never be a better son. You are the best my boy, the bravest.

JAVIER: The Iliad.

HARRY: Poetry, for my son.

*(HARRY gives JAVIER the Purple Heart medal and readjusts blanket. "Namo Amita-bha Buddah" chant begins softly in background. Seeing Harry's united family, LOAN is satisfied that she has fulfilled her mission and exits. Chant becomes louder as lights fade.)*

## END OF PLAY

## TRANSLATION NOTES

## ACT 1, SCENE 2

Giết tôi đi nhưng đừng hãm hại con gái tôi.
Kill me but do not hurt my daughter.

Không! Không! đừng đụng đến con gái tôi.
No, no, do not touch my daughter.

Ối trời ơi! Ôi con gái tôi! Ối trời ơi!
Oh my God! Oh my baby! Oh my God!

Made in the USA
Charleston, SC
19 August 2014